GEOENGINEERING

RESETTING THE THERMOSTAT

EARTH'S CLIMATE

JENNIFER SWANSON

TWENTY-FIRST CENTURY BOOKS / MINNEAPOLIS

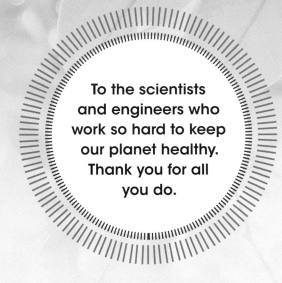

To the scientists
and engineers who
work so hard to keep
our planet healthy.
Thank you for all
you do.

Twenty-First Century Books
A division of Lerner Publishing Group, Inc.
241 First Avenue North
Minneapolis, MN 55401 USA

For reading levels and more information, look up this title at www.lernerbooks.com.

Main body text set in Adobe Garamond Pro 11/15
Typeface provided by Adobe Systems.

Library of Congress Cataloging-in-Publication Data

Names: Swanson, Jennifer.
Title: Geoengineering Earth's climate : resetting the thermostat / Jennifer Swanson.
Description: Minneapolis : Twenty-First Century Books, [2018] | Audience: Age 13–18. |
    Audience: Grade 9 to 12. | Includes bibliographical references and index.
Identifiers: LCCN 2016059722 (print) | LCCN 2017000330 (ebook) | ISBN 9781512415698
    (lb : alk. paper) | ISBN 9781512448641 (eb pdf)
Subjects: LCSH: Environmental engineering. | Climate change mitigation. | Climatic changes. |
    Global warming. | Carbon sequestration.
Classification: LCC TD171.9 .S93 2018 (print) | LCC TD171.9 (ebook) | DDC 551.68—dc23

LC record available at https://lccn.loc.gov/2016059722

Manufactured in the United States of America
1-39926-21392-1/16/2017

CONTENTS

AUTHOR'S NOTE

GEOENGINEERING IS A FASCINATING FIELD OF STUDY.
Some say it is the most important topic of our time. With the effects of climate change creeping into every aspect of our planet, it is easy to see why.

While many geoengineering ideas are controversial, the fact that we are discussing them and researching them shows a collective spirit and one that is interested in resetting Earth's thermostat. I encourage everyone who reads this book to continue learning about this controversial topic. Research. Theorize. Engage in debate. Devise your own ideas if you think you have one that might work. It is the job of the entire planet to solve this issue.

I would also like to thank those leaders in the field who took time out of their busy schedules to speak with me about their projects. The list includes

> Dr. Peter Eisenberger, Global Thermostat
> Dr. Clare Heyward, University of Warwick
> Dr. Richard Houghton, Woods Hole Research Center
> Dr. David Keith, Harvard University
> Dr. Piers Forster, University of Leeds
> Dr. John Sterman, Massachusetts Institute of Technology

They were all happy to share their beliefs and passion for their subjects with me and, by extension, with the readers of this book. I am very grateful to them.

—JENNIFER SWANSON

ONE

AN ABRUPT CHANGE IN CLIMATE

RISING SEAS. Flooded islands. Catastrophic droughts, tornadoes, and hurricanes. Scientists say that these trends, which have been increasing in the twenty-first century, are caused by climate change, created by the warming of Earth. Most scientists also say that humans have caused climate change by burning fossil fuels (coal, petroleum, and natural gas), which release heat-trapping gases into the atmosphere. As levels of these gases increase, the planet grows warmer. The higher temperatures have led to extreme weather events. Most experts agree that if humans don't take action to prevent

Earth from warming further, the climate will undergo even more drastic changes. And these will ultimately affect every living thing on Earth. What can humans do to counteract climate change?

Some engineers propose using geoengineering to tackle the problem. The prefix *geo* means "relating to Earth," so *geoengineering* means "engineering Earth." A more formal definition of *geoengineering* is the "active transformation of Earth's climate through human intervention"—or using technology to reverse the effects of climate change. Sounds good, right? Maybe so. But geoengineering is one of the most complex and controversial topics in the world. Messing with Earth's climate is a big deal and could have lasting consequences, both positive and negative.

CRA-CK!

Tiny cracks have appeared in a glacier (a large body of moving ice) along Evigheds Fjord in western Greenland. In the past, ice and snow completely covered the towering mountains that surround the fjord. But in the twenty-first century, dense rock is visible underneath the ice. The extremely cold weather that allows Greenland's coastal mountains

Chunks of ice break off a glacier on the southeastern coast of Greenland and fall into the Denmark Strait. Warmer air and water temperatures are melting ice in Earth's polar regions, causing sea levels to rise.

to remain covered in ice and snow year-round has changed. Warmer temperatures in Earth's atmosphere are melting the top of the glacier, sending rivulets of ice water into the ocean. Warming waters of the North Atlantic Ocean are melting the glacier from the bottom as well.

The melting glacier on the Evigheds Fjord is part of a much larger formation called an ice sheet. Earth has two major ice sheets—one on Greenland and one on Antarctica. Measuring more than 660,000 square miles (1.7 million square kilometers), Greenland's ice sheet is approximately the size of Texas. On average, the ice sheet is 1 mile (1.6 km) deep. Its greatest depth is 3 miles (4.8 km). If it were to melt entirely, the total amount of water it contains would raise the oceans by about 23 feet (7 meters). The rising waters would flood the coasts of every country on the planet and submerge many inhabited islands.

While the probability of the entire Greenland ice sheet melting is slim, climatologists (scientists who study Earth's climate) note that Greenland is shedding more ice during summer than it regains from snowfall in winter. The US National Aeronautics and Space Administration (NASA) reports that Greenland's ice sheet is losing about 31 billion tons (28 billion metric tons) of ice annually. Some of the melting ice evaporates (turns into water vapor) or stays on the land, but most of it goes directly into the ocean. And studies show that the melting on Greenland is increasing every year.

NASA uses satellites to measure the depth of Earth's oceans. The agency has noticed a definite rise in ocean levels over the last century, with an average yearly rise of about 0.13 inches (3.3 millimeters). While that may seem small, it adds up to a 4- to 8-inch (10- to 20-centimeter) rise over the past one hundred years. If that water were lying in the street, it could flow over curbs and into houses. If you were standing next to the ocean, the rising water would cover your legs to mid-calf. Imagine that much water flooding the entire world. And if the ice sheets continue to melt, the water levels will only get higher.

NASA climate scientist Jay Zwally says that the melting of

NORTH AMERICAN COASTLINES BEFORE AND AFTER PROJECTED MELTING OF EARTH'S ICE

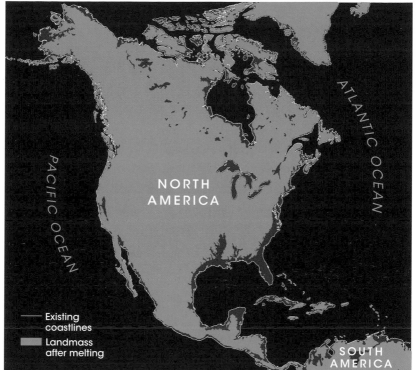

Sea levels have already begun to rise due to global warming. If all the polar ice on Earth were to melt, large areas of coastline would end up underwater. This map shows what North America would look like in that case. Florida would be submerged, along with vast stretches of coast along the Atlantic Ocean and the Gulf of Mexico.

Greenland's ice sheet is like a "canary in a coal mine." Before coal mines used modern air-quality detectors, miners sometimes took live canaries with them into mineshafts. If the birds stopped singing, miners knew that deadly carbon monoxide, which is frequently found inside coal mines, had risen to dangerous levels and killed the birds. Miners then knew it was time to hightail it out of the shaft.

Climatologists think of Greenland as a canary, or an early warning system, for the rest of the planet. Since the Greenland and Antarctic ice sheets account for almost 99 percent of all freshwater ice on the planet,

ICELAND RISING!

The country of Iceland is rising out of the North Atlantic Ocean. No, this scene is not something from a science fiction movie. The land is rising due to climate change. Iceland's rocky terrain is home to many glaciers. The warming waters of the Atlantic Ocean and increasing air temperatures are beginning to melt some of the glaciers.

As the glaciers melt, the land below them rises a little, a phenomenon known as uplift. Imagine a heavy person lying on a mattress, pressing it down. When the person gets up, the mattress bounces up a bit. That's what's happening to the land below Iceland's glaciers. Geologists say that in some places, the uplift rate is 1.2 inches (30 mm) per year.

the melting of either sheet would spell trouble. As Greenland warms and sheds its ice, so do other parts of the Arctic, including Alaska. Many climatologists think that the melted ice streaming into the Arctic Ocean and other northern waters is a signal that the canary has stopped singing. They say that climate change has reached a dire tipping point. Why is this occurring? The answer is related to Earth's atmosphere.

A DELICATE BALANCE

Earth's atmosphere is composed of 78 percent nitrogen and 21 percent oxygen. The remaining 1 percent consists of argon and small amounts of greenhouse gases: methane, nitrous oxide, carbon dioxide, water vapor (water in gas form), and ozone. Greenhouse gases in the atmosphere act like a blanket, holding in heat and shielding Earth from certain kinds of radiation from the sun. When solar energy reaches Earth's atmosphere, about 29 percent of it immediately bounces off clouds and gases and travels back into space. The atmosphere absorbs

another 23 percent, while 48 percent of solar energy makes it to Earth's surface. The land and the oceans absorb this energy and heat up.

The first law of thermodynamics, which applies to everything in the universe, says that energy can neither be created nor destroyed. That means that the amount of energy that goes into a system must equal the amount of energy that the system releases. So on Earth, at the same time the oceans and land are absorbing energy from the sun, they are also releasing energy in the form of infrared rays (heat).

When this heat rises and hits greenhouse gases in the atmosphere, the gases trap the heat and send it back toward Earth. This exchange of energy—from the sun down to Earth's surface, back up to the greenhouse gases, and back down to the ground—naturally keeps Earth at an average temperature of about 59°F (15°C). This is a suitable temperature for life.

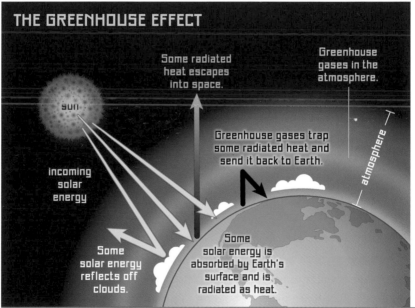

THE GREENHOUSE EFFECT

Some radiated heat escapes into space.

Greenhouse gases in the atmosphere.

sun

Greenhouse gases trap some radiated heat and send it back to Earth.

atmosphere

incoming solar energy

Some solar energy reflects off clouds.

Some solar energy is absorbed by Earth's surface and is radiated as heat.

The greenhouse effect is an exchange of energy that keeps Earth at a suitable temperature for living things. In this exchange, greenhouse gases in the atmosphere trap some of the sun's heat near Earth. However, increasing amounts of greenhouse gases are trapping excessive heat, leading to global climate change.

THE SKY ABOVE US

Meteorologists divide the atmosphere into five layers. The troposphere is the layer closest to Earth. All Earth's wind, rainstorms, and other weather events take place there. The troposphere contains 99 percent of all the water in the atmosphere. This water can become an invisible gas—water vapor. It can become tiny water droplets or ice crystals inside clouds. Or it can fall to Earth as precipitation (rain and snow).

The height of the troposphere varies from place to place. At the equator, the troposphere is 12 miles (19 km) high, but near the North and South Poles it is only 4 miles (6.4 km) high. At the top of the troposphere is a thin layer called the tropopause. It marks the boundary between the troposphere and the layer above it, the stratosphere. Jet airplanes sometimes fly in the stratosphere to stay above any stormy weather below.

At about 9 to 22 miles (15 to 35 km) above Earth's surface, the stratosphere contains a band of gas called the ozone layer. Ozone is a form of oxygen. Whereas an ordinary oxygen molecule has two oxygen atoms, an ozone molecule has three oxygen atoms.

On top of the stratosphere, starting about 31 miles (50 km) above the surface of Earth, is the mesosphere. Above that layer, beginning about 53 miles (85 km) above the planet, is the thermosphere. Beyond that, starting about 429 miles (690 km) above Earth, is the exosphere. It marks the beginning of outer space.

As you go higher into the atmosphere, the concentration of gases gets thinner—the gas molecules are more spread out, with more empty space between them. The air also gets colder as you go higher because there is less gas to trap the sun's heat.

LAYERS OF EARTH'S ATMOSPHERE

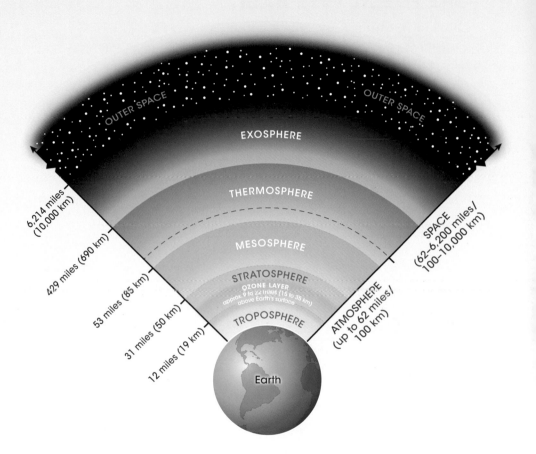

OUTER SPACE

OUTER SPACE

EXOSPHERE

THERMOSPHERE

MESOSPHERE

STRATOSPHERE

OZONE LAYER
approx 9 to 22 miles (15 to 35 km)
above Earth's surface

TROPOSPHERE

Earth

6,214 miles
(10,000 km)

429 miles (690 km)

53 miles (85 km)

31 miles (50 km)

12 miles (19 km)

SPACE
(62–6,200 miles/
100–10,000 km)

ATMOSPHERE
(up to 62 miles/
100 km)

Diagram is not drawn to scale.

The atmosphere is a multilayer blanket of gases around Earth. Because of excess greenhouse gases, the layers nearest the ground are heating up, leading to climate change and extreme weather.

Without greenhouse gases, our planet would be too cold for humans and many other living things. But if levels of greenhouse gases are too high, the planet will get too hot for living things.

THE FOSSIL FUEL HABIT

Since the Industrial Revolution, which began in Europe in the late eighteenth century, humans have been burning fossil fuels to power factories, vehicles, and machinery. Fossil fuels are formed from the remains of long-dead plants and animals—those that lived on Earth hundreds of millions of years ago. After these organisms died, over millions of years, layers of sand and mud accumulated over their bodies. As more layers built up, heat, pressure, and chemical changes turned these remains into fossil fuels: coal, petroleum, and natural gas.

When burned, fossil fuels release carbon dioxide, a greenhouse gas, into Earth's atmosphere. By burning fossil fuels, humans add more than 9 billion tons (8.2 billion metric tons) of carbon dioxide to the atmosphere each year. Along with other greenhouse gases, the excess carbon dioxide causes the atmosphere to trap more heat than it naturally does. So Earth's land and oceans are warming.

The Intergovernmental Panel on Climate Change—a body made up of scientists from around the world—notes that between 1880 and 2016, overall atmospheric carbon dioxide levels increased from 280 parts per million (280 molecules of carbon dioxide for each one million other molecules in the atmosphere) to 400 parts per million (ppm). For the past four thousand years, the amount of carbon dioxide in the atmosphere has hovered steadily around 280 ppm, so this big increase in just 150 years is alarming. Climatologists predict that once carbon dioxide levels reach 450 ppm, melting soil in Arctic regions will release millions of tons of methane, another greenhouse gas. The gas will increase warming further and will melt even more polar ice—an ongoing cycle.

MEET THE GREENHOUSE GASES

Carbon dioxide is a gaseous form of carbon, a chemical element that is found in all living things. Plants take in carbon during photosynthesis—plants using sunlight, carbon dioxide, and water to make energy. Animals take carbon into their bodies when they eat plants. When animals exhale, they release carbon dioxide into the atmosphere. When dead plants and animals decay, they also release carbon dioxide. The movement of carbon dioxide between the atmosphere and living things is called the biological carbon cycle.

Humans have disrupted the biological carbon cycle in two ways. First, they have added excessive carbon dioxide to the atmosphere by burning fossil fuels. Second, they have cut down vast amounts of forests to make room for farms, homes, roads, and ranches. Like other plants, trees pull carbon dioxide from the air and use it during photosynthesis. With fewer trees taking in carbon dioxide, carbon dioxide levels rise even further.

While carbon dioxide makes up more than 75 percent of all the greenhouse gases that humans release into the atmosphere, it isn't the only greenhouse gas on the rise. Methane normally enters the atmosphere when dead plants and animals decay. This process has been going on since life began on Earth. But in the modern era, vast amounts of methane also enter the air from human-made landfills, which contain tons of rotting food, plant waste, and other organic (formerly living) garbage. And livestock such as cattle release methane into the air when they burp and pass gas. A single cow expels 26 to 53 gallons (98 to 201 liters) of methane every day, and Earth is home to more than 1.3 billion cows.

Nitrous oxide levels are also rising due to human activity. Burning fossil fuels releases nitrous oxide into the air, but agriculture accounts for most of the increase. When farmers add nitrogen-based fertilizers to their fields to promote plant growth, bacteria in the soil convert the nitrogen into nitrous oxide. Animal manure, which farmers also use as fertilizer, contains large amounts of nitrous oxide as well.

THE CARBON CYCLE

During the carbon cycle, carbon moves between the atmosphere and Earth continuously, with no starting or stopping point. During the cycle, carbon sometimes leaves the atmosphere. Here are some examples:

- Plants take in carbon dioxide from the air and use it in photosynthesis.
- Some carbon dioxide from the atmosphere dissolves into the ocean.
- In the ocean, organisms that make food via photosynthesis take in carbon dioxide from the air and water.

Carbon also sometimes enters the atmosphere during the carbon cycle. Here are a few examples:

- Animals release carbon dioxide during respiration (breathing).
- When plants and animals die, their tissues decay, releasing carbon dioxide.

Sometimes carbon stalls in the carbon cycle for millions of years. This happens when certain sea creatures die and their bodies drop to the seafloor, piling up in layers of sediment. Over millions of years, the carbon from their bodies turns into fossil fuels (coal, petroleum, and natural gas). It remains buried belowground indefinitely. But humans have altered the carbon cycle by extracting fossil fuels from underground and burning them to power vehicles and machinery. The burning of fossil fuels releases long-buried carbon into the atmosphere, raising carbon levels above normal.

THE BIOLOGICAL AND INDUSTRIAL CARBON CYCLE

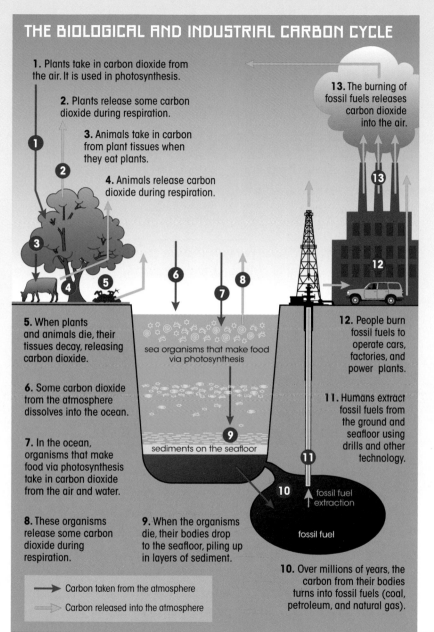

1. Plants take in carbon dioxide from the air. It is used in photosynthesis.

2. Plants release some carbon dioxide during respiration.

3. Animals take in carbon from plant tissues when they eat plants.

4. Animals release carbon dioxide during respiration.

13. The burning of fossil fuels releases carbon dioxide into the air.

5. When plants and animals die, their tissues decay, releasing carbon dioxide.

sea organisms that make food via photosynthesis

12. People burn fossil fuels to operate cars, factories, and power plants.

6. Some carbon dioxide from the atmosphere dissolves into the ocean.

sediments on the seafloor

11. Humans extract fossil fuels from the ground and seafloor using drills and other technology.

7. In the ocean, organisms that make food via photosynthesis take in carbon dioxide from the air and water.

fossil fuel extraction

fossil fuel

8. These organisms release some carbon dioxide during respiration.

9. When the organisms die, their bodies drop to the seafloor, piling up in layers of sediment.

10. Over millions of years, the carbon from their bodies turns into fossil fuels (coal, petroleum, and natural gas).

→ Carbon taken from the atmosphere

⇢ Carbon released into the atmosphere

Carbon moves through the air, land, oceans, and living things in an ongoing cycle. By extracting fossil fuels from belowground and burning them, humans have altered the cycle.

HIGH WATER

Of all the greenhouse gases in the atmosphere, water vapor is the most abundant. It is also the gas that's most involved with rain, snow, hurricanes, and other weather events. That means it plays a crucial role in climate change. As Earth's temperature rises, more liquid water from oceans, lakes, and streams heats up and evaporates. More water vapor traps more heat and causes more warming—a self-perpetuating cycle.

And more water vapor in the air leads to the formation of more clouds and more precipitation. This makes wet areas of the planet wetter, as more water evaporates from Earth's surface and returns to the planet as rain or snow. The extra heat and water in the air also gives more fuel to storms, making them more powerful. Climatologists say that climate change likely intensified some of the most powerful storms to hit the United States in the early twenty-first century, such as Hurricane Katrina in 2005 and Hurricane Sandy in 2012.

Contrary to what you might expect, more water vapor (and other greenhouse gases) in the air can make dry areas of the planet even drier. These places have very little water to begin with, and higher temperatures created by global warming evaporate what little they have. In dry places, the soil can be sunbaked and hard like cement. When rain does fall there, it doesn't soak into the ground to water crops and other plants. Instead, it causes flooding and then quickly runs off the land into waterways.

Increasing droughts (periods of little or no rainfall) and higher temperatures have led to devastating forest fires in many places on Earth. Fires burn hotter and longer when the soil is dry and when dried-up dead vegetation sits on the land. The dry vegetation acts like kindling, providing fires with lots of fuel. Powerful fires devoured vast areas of wilderness in the western United States in the second decade of the twenty-first century. Climatologists say that climate change led to the dry and hot conditions that fueled the fires. And forest fires add even more heat-trapping carbon into the air, increasing warming further.

TIME TO ACT

Earth is already feeling the effects of excess greenhouse gases in the atmosphere. The heating up of air and the oceans has changed normal climate patterns, leading to violent storms, extreme droughts, record-breaking high temperatures, and melting ice sheets and glaciers. The changes are hurting animals, plants, and humans. For instance, the melting of glaciers is destroying the habitats (natural homes) of ice-dwelling animals such as polar bears. Rising water has flooded coastal areas worldwide, destroying the homes of people, plants, and animals. Warming ocean waters have killed corals and other sea life.

Drought in the African nation of Namibia has killed trees and dried out the soil. Climate scientists say that droughts will increase as Earth continues to warm.

Experts say that to halt climate change, humans must greatly reduce the amount of carbon they release into the atmosphere. But doing so would not immediately lower carbon levels or global temperatures. John D. Sterman, a professor of system dynamics at the Massachusetts Institute of Technology near Boston, uses a simple visual image to explain increasing levels of carbon in the atmosphere.

THE SUNNY SIDE

The sun's temperature is not constant. It changes over time. Could this fluctuation be causing warming on Earth? Climate scientists say no. According to National Aeronautics and Space Administration (NASA), since 1750, the average amount of energy coming from the sun has increased only slightly, a change that's inconsistent with the amount of warming happening on Earth. In other words, Earth is hotter than it should be. And climate scientists say that if a hotter sun were to blame for a warmer Earth, all layers of Earth's atmosphere would be warming. But warming is taking place only in the lower layers of the atmosphere, where greenhouse gases are trapping heat near the ground.

He describes a bathtub with the faucet flowing and with the drain at the bottom left unplugged. In this scenario, the bathtub represents Earth's atmosphere. The water pouring from the tap represents carbon that humans are adding to the atmosphere by burning fossil fuels and cutting down forests. The water swirling down the drain is carbon that leaves the atmosphere naturally, via photosynthesis and other processes. But even with the drain unplugged, more water flows into the bathtub than leaves it.

The meaning of Sterman's bathtub image is that even if we could turn off the tap of incoming carbon emissions completely, carbon dioxide levels would still be too high, and Earth would still be too warm. University of Chicago climatologist David Archer says that it would take hundreds of years for the extra carbon added by humans to swirl down the drain, returning Earth to preindustrial levels. Hundreds of years is too long to wait, most climate scientists say. To save our planet for future generations, humans need to find ways to reduce the threat immediately. That's where geoengineering comes into the picture.

TWO

TIME TO GET SERIOUS

OFF THE NORTHEASTERN COAST OF AUSTRALIA, BELOW THE SURFACE OF THE PACIFIC OCEAN, IS THE BREATHTAKING GREAT BARRIER REEF, OFTEN CALLED ONE OF THE SEVEN NATURAL WONDERS OF THE WORLD. This limestone formation was constructed by animals called stony corals. Their bodies are brightly colored in vivid shades of red, yellow, orange, blue, or green, depending on the species. Each individual coral, or coral polyp, has a limestone skeleton around the lower half of its body. The skeleton grows together with the skeletons of dead and other living coral polyps, creating a rigid structure called a reef. The Great Barrier Reef contains more than three thousand individual reefs stretching for more than 1,800 miles (3,000 km). Besides corals, the reef is home to thousands of species of tropical fish, turtles, sea snakes, starfish, clams, whales, dolphins, marine plants, and other aquatic life. Yet many of the reef's corals are dying.

Coral polyps have a mutualistic (mutually beneficial) relationship with a type of algae called zooxanthellae. The algae live in the bodies of coral polyps. The polyps give the algae a safe home and some of the materials they need to carry out photosynthesis. In exchange, during photosynthesis, the algae produce substances vital to coral, including oxygen and compounds used to make food and to build stony skeletons.

Changing environmental conditions—such as warming waters, cooling waters, or excess carbon dioxide in the water—can stress coral polyps. This stress leads them to expel the algae they rely on. Without this source of food and oxygen, the normally colorful polyps bleach, or turn white. Eventually they die.

Fish and other sea creatures make their homes in the Great Barrier Reef, a series of coral formations off the coast of northeastern Australia. Warming ocean waters and excess carbon dioxide in the water are harming corals and the plants and animals that live with them.

A coral reef is a complex ecosystem—a community of living things that depend on one another for food and reproduction. For instance, many fish that live along coral reefs eat coral polyps and the plants and sea creatures that live with them. Many fish and other sea animals lay eggs in the sheltered cracks and crevices of coral reefs. When coral polyps begin to die, the entire ecosystem starts to fall apart. The plants and animals there have less food to eat. And the same environmental changes that can damage corals, such as excess carbon dioxide in the water, can also damage other members of the ecosystem.

In the twenty-first century, large portions of the Great Barrier Reef and Earth's other ocean reefs are bleaching and dying. Biologists say that warming ocean waters and excess carbon dioxide in the water are to blame. And the situation is far from unique. Around the globe, higher air temperatures and increasing levels of carbon dioxide are threatening thousands of plant and animal species. How might humans halt—or at least lessen—this kind of damage caused by climate change?

INCOMPLETE SOLUTIONS

Experts agree that the best way to fight climate change is to cut back on the use of fossil fuels. This isn't an easy task, though. Did you take the bus or a car to school today? Chances are, that vehicle burned gasoline, which is derived from petroleum, a fossil fuel. Feeling hot? You might turn on a fan or an air conditioner. Both of these run on electricity, and to make that electricity, power plants often burn coal or natural gas—fossil fuels. Feeling cold? You can turn on a heater. It might run on electricity, or it might burn petroleum or natural gas. In 2015 fossil fuels provided more than 67 percent of the energy used in the United States. Approximately 86 percent of the world's energy used comes from fossil fuels.

Some individuals, governments, and businesses are trying to reduce fossil fuel emissions by adopting "green," or environmentally friendly, policies and technologies. Mainly this involves switching to alternative energy technology, such as wind power, solar power, waterpower, and

In the United States and other industrialized nations, most people rely on cars for transportation. The majority of cars run on gasoline, which comes from petroleum, a fossil fuel. Experts say that to reduce the amount of carbon dioxide in the atmosphere, we must cut down on fossil fuel use. Electric cars are an alternative.

geothermal power. These technologies provide energy without the use of fossil fuels. For instance, solar systems collect energy from the sun and use it to produce heat and electricity. Windmills and wind turbines spin around with air currents, and this spinning motion can generate electrical power. Similarly, the movement of ocean waves and water flowing over dams or waterfalls can power electric generators. Geothermal systems pump hot water or steam from deep inside Earth and use it to power electric generators.

The fossil fuels we use in modern times took hundreds of millions of years to form. Once these fuels are gone, they're gone—unless we want to wait hundreds of millions of years for new ones to form. Alternative fuels, on the other hand, are called renewable energy sources. A renewable energy source replaces itself naturally or never runs out. For instance, wind is a renewable energy source because the wind blows again and again. You can't use up the wind. The sun has been shining for 4.6 billion years and will continue to shine for another 5 billion years—probably longer than humans will live on Earth. Biomass—or plant materials that are burned for fuel—are also renewable, since people can grow new plants to replace those they burn.

Is the switch to alternative and renewable fuels helping in the fight against climate change? Yes and no. According to a report from the National Renewable Energy Laboratory (NREL, an agency of the US Department of Energy), Americans are getting more and more of their electricity from renewables like wind and solar power. In 2004 only 9.5 percent of the nation's electricity came from renewable power sources. By 2013 the percentage was 14.8, with wind power accounting for most of that increase. Between 2000 and 2013, the amount of electricity generated from renewable fuels more than doubled. Around the world, renewable fuels accounted for 23 percent of all electrical generation in 2013. Both China and the United States, the world's largest consumers of energy, are building wind power facilities at a fast clip. Solar energy is also skyrocketing in the United States, China, and Japan.

Wind power doesn't add carbon dioxide or other greenhouse gases to the atmosphere.

But the NREL report also notes that "while renewable and alternative fuels (including electric vehicles) are growing fast, they're still minuscule compared to petroleum-based fuels." And renewable energy is not cheap. Sun and wind power come to us free of charge, but we need solar panels, wind turbines, and a lot of other equipment to turn that power into electricity or heat and to transport it to those who need it. Building and installing all that equipment costs money, and the costs get passed on to consumers. For example, according to the US Department of Energy, it costs 24 cents to produce one kilowatt-hour of energy from a solar thermal (heat) power system but only 7 to 14 cents to produce one kilowatt-hour of energy from natural gas. Since the typical US household uses 10,932 kilowatt-hours of energy per year, the difference in cost between fossil fuels and alternatives can amount to hundreds or thousands of dollars a year, making it uneconomical to switch. (Some alternative fuels are cheaper than others, though, and as more alternative energy facilities are built and the technology improves, prices will likely come down.)

So while alternative and renewable fuels are helping in the fight against climate change, they are not making much of a dent in fossil fuel consumption. It takes a long time (and a lot of money) for power grids, businesses, and homeowners to switch to alternative energy and an even longer time for the changes to create a noticeable impact on the atmosphere. Climate scientists worry that time is running out. They estimate that Earth's temperature has already increased 1.5°F (0.8°C) since the preindustrial age. They say it could reach the 3.6°F (2°C) mark by 2050—a change that would be disastrous for the planet.

Beyond switching to alternative fuels, what can humans do to fight climate change? Some say that geoengineering is the answer. Climatologists and engineers could create large-scale technologies to interfere with Earth's existing systems, such as the biological carbon cycle, in ways that would counteract climate change. This is a radical idea but one that just might work—and work quickly.

HOW WILL IT WORK?

One of the primary goals of geoengineering is to physically remove carbon dioxide from the atmosphere. A drastic reduction in carbon dioxide might bring global temperatures back to safe levels. Geoengineers have identified several different methods of doing this. One of them is reforestation, which means planting large forests. The trees in these forests would capture large amounts of carbon during photosynthesis. Another approach is carbon capture and sequestration (CCS)—giant machines would pull carbon dioxide from the atmosphere and the carbon would be sequestered (isolated) somewhere, such as underground.

Besides removing carbon from the air, geoengineers could try to lower Earth's temperature by allowing less sunlight to reach the ground. Some engineers propose creating large clouds to reflect sunlight away from Earth and back into space. Others want to place giant mirrors into orbit. These would also reflect sunlight away from Earth. With less solar radiation reaching Earth, greenhouse gases would trap less heat from the sun.

Capturing carbon, reflecting sunlight, and other ideas to fight climate change are based in scientific theory, but humans haven't put any of the methods into widespread use. Geoengineering is a relatively new science, with only limited testing to back up the important results it might be able to deliver. And as with all major actions, messing with global climate systems comes with big risks. For example, if humans interfere with Earth's climate by removing carbon from the atmosphere or deflecting sunlight away from Earth, might this create even more droughts, floods, and other weather extremes beyond those we're already seeing? And if we change the climate in one part of the world, how will that impact the climate in another part of the world?

THE FIRST GEOENGINEERS

Since geoengineering is the large-scale manipulation of the climate, one could argue that humans have been unintentionally geoengineering Earth's climate for centuries. Since the Industrial Revolution, we have been burning fossil fuels and cutting down forests, both of which increase atmospheric carbon levels and lead to climate change. You could say that the climate we have in the twenty-first century was created through geoengineering.

And although the term *geoengineering* emerged in the twenty-first century, humans have been intentionally geoengineering the climate since the mid-twentieth century. In 1946 the General Electric Research Laboratory in Schenectady, New York, sent a plane to seed a cloud. Seeding a cloud means adding something to it to create precipitation. In this case, meteorologist (weather and atmosphere scientist) Vincent Schaefer, who accompanied the pilot on the flight, released 3 pounds (1.4 kilograms) of frozen carbon dioxide (also called dry ice) into a cloud. His goal was to produce snow, and he did. Schaefer later noted that he "was thrilled to see long streamers of snow falling from the base of the cloud through which we had just passed." He had just created the first human-made snowstorm.

The US government was excited about cloud seeding. With this ability, it could create precipitation where and when it was needed. Need rain in the drought-stricken Southwest? Done. Want to make heavy rain in an enemy nation to destroy its coffee crop? Done. Some government officials viewed the power to seed clouds as a brand-new weapon.

In August 1953, the US government formed the Advisory Committee on Weather Control. Its goal was to investigate the effectiveness of weather-altering and to determine if the United States should do so. At the time, the United States and the Soviet Union (a nation of fifteen republics that included Russia) were bitter enemies. But meteorologists from the two nations discussed ways to change the weather worldwide. One idea was to release huge amounts of dust into the stratosphere to bring rain to drought-stricken farming areas. The Soviet Union even considered building dams across the Bering Strait, a body of water between Russia and Alaska, to redirect Pacific

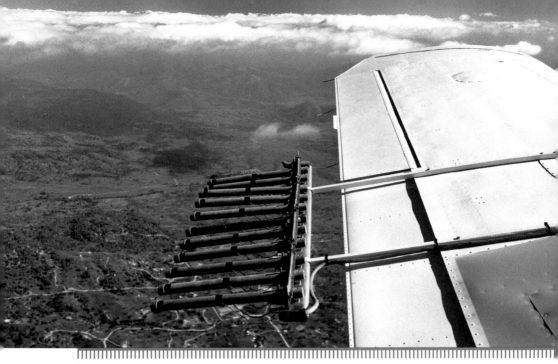

Although cloud seeding can have unintended results, governments and businesses sometimes use it to create precipitation. This photograph shows an airplane wing equipped with jets for spraying silver iodide, which can trigger clouds to make rain or snow.

Ocean currents. The goal was to make the Northern Hemisphere warmer and to melt ice in the Arctic Ocean, thus opening up a new route for cargo ships.

In the following decades, government groups, businesses, and universities sometimes used cloud seeding to bring rain to US farmland. But a 1972 federal-government-led cloud-seeding project in South Dakota resulted in a disastrous flood. Angry farmers then sued the government. By then meteorologists had learned that weather modification was not easy to control. For example, you could seed a cloud in one place, but the rain might end up many miles away, where rain was not necessarily needed.

Still, the US government felt that weather modification might be a good weapon. During the Vietnam War (1957–1975), a conflict in Southeast Asia, the US military secretly seeded clouds over the Ho Chi Minh Trail in Laos, a supply line for enemy troops.

CLEARING THE SKIES

How do you ensure great weather when you are hosting one of the most famous athletic competitions in the world? You seed the clouds overhead to control the rain. That is exactly what China did prior to the opening ceremony of the 2008 Olympics in Beijing.

When a large thunderstorm threatened to put a damper on the event, Chinese technicians fired eleven hundred rockets filled with silver iodide into the air. The project lasted more than four hours and took place at twenty-one different sites in the city. The particles of silver iodide triggered the formation of ice pellets in clouds. The ice fell to Earth in the form of rain.

But the rain didn't fall on Beijing. The meteorologists who carried out the cloud seeding studied weather patterns and designed the project to produce rain elsewhere. The rain shower that resulted dropped 4 inches (10 cm) of precipitation in the city of Baoding, about 93 miles (150 km) southwest of Beijing, while the capital city remained dry.

A Chinese artillery operator stands near a gun used to fire cloud-seeding rockets into the atmosphere. Before the 2008 Olympics in Beijing, China, the Beijing Meteorological Bureau fired hundreds of such rockets. The project kept the skies clear over Beijing and the Olympic venues while bringing rain to a city nearby.

The United States wanted to increase rainfall and turn the trail into mud to make travel there difficult. The effort was successful in bogging down movements of enemy troops and supplies over several years. But when news of the operation leaked to the press, Americans were concerned. Many felt that altering the weather in foreign nations was unfair. It could bring ruin to farmers and others who relied on predictable seasonal weather patterns. Citizens of other nations agreed, and in 1976, the United Nations, an international humanitarian and peacekeeping body, outlawed unfriendly or aggressive weather modification technology.

INTO THE FUTURE

In the twenty-first century, climate scientists use powerful computers to model their geoengineering ideas. But they can't know for sure if the ideas will work in the real world. And geoengineering is still highly controversial. More than thirty years after banning weather modification after the Vietnam War, in 2010 the United Nations banned geoengineering in general because it could have unintended consequences. For instance, it could change weather patterns, bringing more rain to one region while reducing it elsewhere. Reduced rainfall could lead to droughts, which in turn could bring about crop failure and then famine. And instead of keeping Earth from getting warmer, geoengineering might make Earth too cold. It could lead to a new ice age, with temperatures far too low for the survival of many plant and animal species. Finally, some nations might use geoengineering as a weapon, deliberately creating floods or droughts in enemy nations, destroying crops and potentially leading to starvation of a civilian population.

While acknowledging the risks of geoengineering, climatologists caution that doing nothing to counteract increasing global temperatures could be just as harmful as geoengineering itself. So humans are stuck at a crossroads. Resetting the global thermostat is becoming a vital need. Geoengineering theoretically will do that, but at what cost? Will the reward be worth it? Only time will tell, and yet time also may be running out.

THREE

CAPTURING CARBON

COUGH. *Cough. Cough.* Standing at your open door, you wipe your hand across your watery eyes. You cough again as you inhale thick, hazy air, and your throat becomes dry and tickly. Your eyes sting and your nose wrinkles as it encounters the foul smell of car exhaust and other pollution.

You are in a city with some of the unhealthiest air in the world: Beijing, China. Not all days are as bad as this one. On some days, depending on the wind direction, the air over Beijing is mostly clear and sun shines across the beautiful skyline. But on other days, when the wind shifts, air pollution from nearby industrial plants blows into the city and hovers overhead. The dark haze makes it difficult to see, swallowing up the tops of buildings, cars, and even people. On days like that, the air quality index (AQI), a measure of the amount of pollution in the air, can reach as high as 300 to 500. This means there are 300 to 500 micrograms of particulate pollution (tiny particles and liquid droplets) in every 35 cubic feet (1 cu. m) of air. Compare that to a healthy AQI reading, which is 0 to 50.

Beijing is not the only city with pollution problems. Los Angeles, California; Delhi, India; Jubail, Saudi Arabia; and many other cities have high levels of air pollution. But Beijing has some of the worst pollution on Earth. The mountains that surround the city form a container that holds in polluted air. On the worst days in Beijing, the AQI tops 700.

Some of the air pollution comes from industrial plants, and some of it comes from cars. By burning fossil fuels, factories and cars release

In Tiananmen Square in Beijing, a young woman uses her smartphone while military guards stand at attention. In Beijing thick smog often limits visibility and most city dwellers wear face masks to reduce the amount of pollution entering their lungs.

carbon monoxide, hydrocarbons, nitrous oxide, and other gases into the air. The particulates, or tiny particles, in these gases mix with moisture in the air to form smog, a name combining the words *smoke* and *fog*. Sometimes sunlight reacts with hydrocarbons and nitrous oxide to form ozone and other gases, a type of pollution called photochemical smog. Both types of smog can irritate people's noses, eyes, and throats and damage their lungs. People who are regularly exposed to high levels of air pollution can develop asthma, emphysema, and heart problems. Extremely heavy smog can kill plants and even humans. On smoggy days, many of the seventeen million residents of Beijing wear masks over their mouths and noses to reduce the amount of pollution entering their lungs.

Health officials in Beijing and elsewhere recommend that citizens stay inside on smoggy days and use air purifiers to clean indoor air. This is not a permanent fix, however. It doesn't clean up pollution, and it doesn't reduce the amount of heat-trapping carbon dioxide entering the atmosphere. Switching to renewable and alternative fuels—such as solar power, wind power, and hydropower—is a step in the right direction. These energy sources don't add more carbon to the air—but they don't remove it from the air either. And that's exactly what some scientists think we need to do to fight climate change: actively remove excess carbon dioxide from the air.

IF A TREE FALLS IN THE FOREST

A natural way to pull carbon dioxide from the air is with reforestation, or planting forests full of trees. Whether it's a tropical rain forest in South America, a dense forest of evergreens in Canada, or stands of redwoods in California—any type of forest will capture carbon. That's because trees, like all plants, absorb carbon dioxide during photosynthesis.

Besides absorbing carbon dioxide, healthy forests are vital ecosystems—communities of living and nonliving things that interact with and depend on one another. Thousands of species of plants live in forests. Thousands of species of animals make their homes, raise

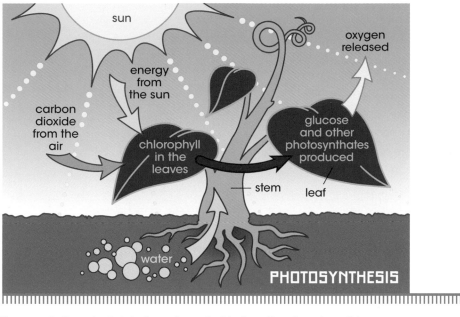

energy
from
the sun

sun

oxygen
released

carbon
dioxide
from the
air

chlorophyll
in the
leaves

glucose
and other
photosynthates
produced

stem   leaf

water

PHOTOSYNTHESIS

Trees and other plants take in carbon dioxide from the air and use it to make energy. Widespread deforestation has reduced the number of trees absorbing carbon dioxide this way. We could reverse this process and reduce atmospheric carbon dioxide levels by planting trees to replace those that have been destroyed.

their young, and find food inside forests. Forest trees protect the soil by sending their roots deep into the ground. The networks of roots hold the soil in place and prevent it from eroding, or washing away, during rainstorms. Trees also capture rainwater in their leaves, which keeps excess water from hitting the ground and causing floods. Trees play a crucial part in Earth's water cycle as well. Water from the soil enters trees through their roots, moves through their trunks and branches, and evaporates from their leaves. The water eventually returns to the forest soil as rain and snow and begins its cycle again.

Forests also play a significant role in human society. Did you read a book or newspaper today? Pin papers onto a cork bulletin board? Blow your nose? If so, you used a product derived from a tree. Manufacturers use wood from trees to make paper and facial tissue. They create many

THE WATER CYCLE

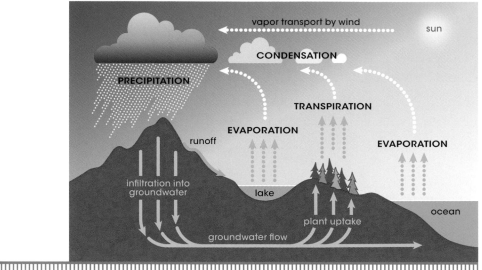

By taking up groundwater through their roots and releasing it through their leaves, trees play a key role in Earth's water cycle. Deforestation has disrupted this cycle and also increased atmospheric carbon dioxide levels.

medicines, cosmetics, waxes, oils, and other products from the leaves, bark, and sap of trees.

Even though trees are valuable to humans, forests are disappearing at an alarming rate. Since the mid-twentieth century, loggers have cut down more than half of the world's forests. According to the United Nations Food and Agriculture Organization, people destroy almost 18 million acres (7.3 million hectares) of forests each year. That's about the size of Panama or about half the size of Illinois. It equals approximately thirty-six football fields full of trees destroyed every day. Humans cut down trees for many reasons: to create products from wood, leaves, and bark; to build roads through forested land; and to make room for houses, farms, and ranches.

When humans cut down trees, they don't just destroy forest ecosystems. They also change the carbon cycle. Forests are a type of carbon sink, a natural system that removes carbon from the atmosphere and stores it. Oceans, soil, and fields full of plants are also carbon sinks. According to the US Forest Service, American forests absorb enough carbon to offset between 10 and 20 percent of all US fossil fuel emissions per year. The more forests we have on Earth, the more carbon dioxide they remove from the air. But that also works in reverse. The more trees we cut down, the less carbon dioxide trees can remove from the air. With more heat-trapping carbon dioxide in the air, the more global temperatures rise.

The rain forest surrounding the Amazon River and its tributaries (feeder rivers) in South America covers an immense 2 million square miles (5.2 million sq. km) of land. The Amazon rain forest is one of the largest carbon sinks in the world.

But between 1978 and 2016, humans destroyed more than 289,000 square miles (749,000 sq. km) of Amazon rain forest to build roads and farms, to harvest wood, and to mine for minerals under the soil. This rapid elimination of the rain forest released massive amounts of heat-trapping carbon into the atmosphere, accelerating climate change. And destruction of large numbers of

DOES A CARBON RISE HELP TREES?

After large areas of forest are cut, leaving fewer trees to carry out photosynthesis, carbon dioxide levels rise. Studies have shown that the extra carbon helps the remaining trees in the forest grow faster and higher. That makes sense, since carbon dioxide is vital to plant growth. But the extra carbon is not really a benefit for the trees. They actually grow too quickly. During this quick growth, they don't establish the extensive roots systems developed by trees that grow more slowly, which makes them more vulnerable to drought. So the trees die younger than those that absorb normal amounts of carbon. And because they have shorter life spans, they remove less carbon from the air.

Since the late 1970s, humans have destroyed vast sections of the Amazon rain forest. Areas cleared of trees, such as this one in Peru, can no longer function as carbon sinks.

trees hurt the forest ecosystem. With fewer trees to capture rainwater, prevent erosion, and take part in the water cycle, parts of the forest began to dry out.

For many years, environmentalists have been sounding the alarm about destruction of the Amazon rain forest. In 2004 governments of nations that are home to the rain forest—Ecuador, Peru, Bolivia, and Brazil—started taking steps to protect it. They began limiting the numbers of trees that could be cut, declaring some areas off-limits to logging, and planting new trees to replace those cut down.

Will these efforts help prevent climate change? According to Dr. Richard Houghton, an ecologist at the Woods Hole Research Center in Massachusetts, the answer is a resounding yes. Houghton believes that simply stopping deforestation in Earth's tropical regions would have monumental impact. For example, if the approximately 31.5 million acres (12.8 million hectares) of trees currently being cut down in tropical regions each year were instead left intact, they would absorb

1.1 to 2.2 billion tons (1 to 2 billion metric tons) of carbon per year. As they grew, they would absorb even more carbon per year, between 1.1 and 3.3 billion tons (1 to 3 billion metric tons). Moreover, if trees could be replanted on the more than 1.2 billion acres (500 million hectares) previously deforested by humans, those trees would absorb another 1.1 billion tons of carbon per year. Do the math:

- 1.1 to 2.2 billion tons from not cutting down trees +
- 1.1 to 3.3 billion tons if the trees that are not cut down are allowed to grow to maturity +
- 1.1 billion tons from replanting the previously decimated 1.2 billion acres.

The result is absorption of between 3.3 and 6.6 billion tons (3 to 6 billion metric tons) of carbon per year. Houghton summarizes: "That's equivalent to *30–60% of current emissions of carbon from fossil fuel use.*" The numbers show that humans could make a significant dent in global carbon emissions—and potentially slow climate change—by eliminating deforestation and implementing widespread reforestation.

Yet many governments and businesses are reluctant to halt deforestation. Loggers cut down trees so that businesses can make products that consumers want to buy. For instance, palm trees produce palm oil, which is used to make thousands of products—everything from snack foods to shampoos to ice cream. Because palm oil is a big moneymaker for many companies, loggers continue to cut down palm trees. Businesses aren't likely to stop practices that make them a lot of money, but as the perils of climate change have become more apparent, attitudes are starting to change. For example, to help fight climate change, major food companies such as Hershey and Kellogg's have announced they will buy palm oil only from palm tree plantations that practice reforestation.

Schools, governments, and nonprofit organizations have also begun reforestation efforts. In Brazil the Planeterra Foundation planted more than 450,000 trees from 2009 to 2012. The organization continues to work with Trees for the Future (TFTF), a US-based reforestation program that has been planting trees in Brazil since 1989. And students in many parts of Africa and South America have joined school-based reforestation programs, raising tree saplings for three to five years until they are strong enough for replanting. Students learn the importance of forests as carbon sinks and study how strong tree root systems can prevent erosion and reduce flooding. They also learn eco-friendly planting and harvesting methods along with ways to promote biodiversity, or the growth of many different plants and animal species in the same ecosystem.

These efforts are a start. But as Houghton's numbers show, it will take more than voluntary programs to significantly offset carbon emissions from fossil fuels. It will take wide-scale, global reforestation efforts to make a difference.

A young man tends to mahogany tree seedlings at a nursery in Brazil. With widespread reforestation efforts, groups hope to reduce atmospheric carbon dioxide levels and also restore forest ecosystems.

CARBON-NEUTRAL BIOMASS

Humans can also fight climate change—or at least keep it from getting worse—by using plant-based biomass fuels. Plant biomass includes leaves, sticks, grass, wood chips, and bark taken from recently living plants and trees. Because plants practice photosynthesis and absorb carbon dioxide, all these materials contain carbon. When biomass is burned as fuel, it releases this carbon back into the atmosphere.

Wait a minute! Fossil fuels also come from formerly living organisms and also release carbon dioxide when they are burned. So why is biomass more eco-friendly? It's a matter of time. When we burn biomass plants, we release carbon that was recently removed from the atmosphere—during photosynthesis taking place when the plants that provided the biomass were alive. With biomass, the amounts of carbon taken from the atmosphere and the amount released back into the atmosphere cancel each other out. This makes biomass carbon neutral. Fossil fuels, on the other hand, removed their carbon dioxide from the atmosphere millions of years ago. When we burn them, nothing in existing natural processes offsets the extra carbon they release. So fossil fuels are not carbon neutral but instead add carbon to the total amount in the atmosphere.

FROM CARBON NEUTRAL TO CARBON NEGATIVE

Since biomass fuels are carbon neutral, they don't actually reduce the amount of carbon dioxide in the air. But some engineers envision a system called bioenergy with carbon capture and sequestration (BECCS) that would capture the carbon released by biomass fuels and sequester it, removing it from the carbon cycle and thus making a dent in climate change.

Here's how such a system would work. First, farmers grow trees, which are then cut down and cut up into tiny wooden pellets. Power plants burn the pellets to spin turbines that generate electricity.

BIOCHAR

Besides fighting climate change, biomass might benefit agriculture. Here's how. When biomass is burned in a power plant, it leaves behind charred remains similar to charcoal. This material, biochar, is very porous—it readily absorbs fluids. Biochar takes centuries to break down into tiny particles.

Some environmentalists propose placing large amounts of biochar on farm fields, where it will absorb rainwater, keep the soil moist, and help crops grow. And the carbon inside biochar will remain there, not moving into the atmosphere to increase carbon levels.

But from a geoengineering standpoint, biochar has some drawbacks. It is very dark, and dark colors absorb heat. Have you ever noticed that in hot places, people tend to wear white clothing? That's because white reflects the sun's heat, and people dressed in white feel cooler than those dressed in black or another dark color. So vast fields of dark biochar would absorb a lot of heat, adding to Earth's warming.

Finally, the sheer act of burning biomass to make biochar, transporting it in fossil-fuel-burning vehicles, and placing it into the soil with fossil-fuel-burning machines will create extra carbon emissions. Any large-scale geoengineering project involving biochar will need to grapple with these issues and make a convincing case that the pros outweigh the cons.

Some people propose using large amounts of biochar, or the remains of burned biomass, to hold moisture and trap carbon in the soil. But because it is black, biochar absorbs heat, so it could worsen global warming.

A truck unloads wood chips at a biomass warehouse in the United Kingdom. When the trees that provided the chips were alive, they absorbed carbon dioxide during photosynthesis. When the chips are burned for fuel, they will release that carbon dioxide. The process is carbon neutral, since the amount of carbon released cancels out the amount of carbon absorbed. But if machinery captures the carbon dioxide when the chips are burned, the process is carbon negative.

As the pellets burn, machinery captures the carbon dioxide in the emissions and compresses it. (Compressing gas reduces its volume, making it easier to transport and handle.) The compressed gas can be stored long-term in large tanks or sold to businesses that use carbon dioxide in manufacturing. Such businesses include beer and soda companies, which use carbon dioxide to add fizz to their beverages; greenhouses that use the gas to promote plant growth; and companies that turn carbon dioxide into fertilizer and dry ice. BECCS would be carbon negative—it would remove more carbon from the atmosphere (through the growth of biomass and the capturing of carbon) than would be released into the atmosphere when the biomass is burned.

Can biomass become a long-term, sustainable alternative fossil fuel? Energy expert Daniel Kammen of the University of California–Berkeley believes so. He states, "Biomass, if managed sustainably can provide the 'sink' for carbon that, if utilized in concert with low-carbon generation technologies, can enable us to reduce carbon in the atmosphere."

CARBON CAPTURE

While no BECCS plants are in the works, some companies are making plans to capture carbon from power plants that burn fossil fuels. For example, the Petra Nova Carbon Capture Project, a joint venture between the US Department of Energy and private industry, will capture carbon from a coal-burning power plant in Houston, Texas. The project is designed to capture 90 percent of the carbon dioxide from the plant's emissions. That carbon dioxide will then be compressed and shipped to oil fields in the Houston area, where it will be used to help release oil from old oil wells.

Capturing carbon from power plants is straightforward because so much carbon is concentrated in power plant emissions. But some geoengineering pioneers want to capture carbon directly from the air around us. This is much harder. The carbon dioxide in power plant emissions can be as much as 700 ppm, whereas in plain old air, carbon levels are about 400 ppm. That makes finding the carbon dioxide among the millions of other gas molecules in the air (including oxygen, nitrogen, and methane) far more difficult.

A revolutionary process called direct carbon capture (DCC) can rise to the challenge. A DCC company called Global Thermostat, founded in 2010, has built a prototype carbon capture system that pulls carbon dioxide out of the air anywhere outside. The system consists of 10-foot-wide (3 m) platforms—called contactors—that sit on top of a 40-foot-high (12 m) tower. The tower can be raised and lowered as needed. Up in the air, giant fans inside the tower suck masses of air across the contactors. Chemicals in the contactors then pull carbon dioxide in the air. The collected carbon dioxide is compressed and then sent by pipes to a permanent storage site or to industries that use carbon dioxide in manufacturing.

Between 2008 and 2013, a test facility in Ketzin, Germany, accepted more than 67,000 tons (61,000 metric tons) of carbon dioxide for storage in underground units. A German research organization operated the facility to explore the viability of carbon capture and sequestration.

Existing DCC systems capture about 40,000 tons (36,287 metric tons) of carbon dioxide every year. That's only about 0.01 percent of the carbon dioxide produced worldwide. We'd need thousands of DCC systems to make even a small dent in the reduction of carbon emissions. But Dr. Peter Eisenberger of Global Thermostat is optimistic about the future of DDC. He has contacted industries that rely on carbon dioxide, such as soft-drink companies, oil companies, and greenhouses. Eisenberger thinks that by selling the carbon dioxide to these businesses, he can make DCC profitable, scale up the business to include thousands of carbon-capture machines, and help fight climate change.

In the future, Global Thermostat and other carbon capture businesses might have even more buyers for the carbon they collect. The Houston-based power company NRG Energy announced in 2015 that it would offer a $20 million prize to teams of engineers who can devise systems for turning carbon captured from coal- and gas-burning power plants into useful products. Forty-seven teams are vying for the award, which is called the Carbon XPrize. What kind of products might be made from captured carbon? Ideas include plastics, baking soda, vehicle fuels, cement, and foam for sneakers, couch cushions, and automobile seats. NRG explains that the carbon-based products will store carbon just like trees, oceans, and soil do, thereby keeping it out of the atmosphere. The company will choose the winning team in 2020.

PROS AND CONS

Carbon removal systems have both benefits and drawbacks. Reforestation has important benefits for the environment because it restores forest ecosystems. On the negative side, reforestation is expensive and can take a long time to show results. Creating networks for capturing, transporting, and storing carbon also takes time and money. It requires building carbon-capture facilities, carbon-storage sites, and pipes to carry the carbon there. All this construction could harm the environment, since it likely would involve machinery and vehicles that run on fossil fuels and might require cutting down trees and thus destroying plant and animal habitats. An alternative to building extensive carbon pipelines would be to build carbon-capture plants next to carbon storage sites. This construction would also be quite costly, but it would save on piping and transportation costs. Most engineers think that underground storage sites make the most sense for captured carbon, since they don't take up space aboveground, freeing up the land for other uses. But constructing such storage units would still disrupt natural environments and perhaps aquifers (underground water reservoirs).

Removing carbon from the atmosphere has negatives, including a high cost. But government and business leaders must weigh those negatives against the big positive: that removing carbon might perhaps save Earth from unlivable high temperatures.

FOUR

ROCK AND ROLL

ROCKS ARE EVERYWHERE. Mountains are made of rocks. Rocks sit at the bottom of rivers and along coastlines. They litter the ground in many places. Construction companies use rocks to make houses and other buildings. And some geologists think humans can use rocks to fight climate change. That's because some rocks are natural carbon sinks. They hold carbon inside them for millions of years.

Rocks are part of the geological carbon cycle. In this cycle, carbon moves from the air to the land and oceans. From the oceans, some carbon moves deep inside Earth.

These limestone formations, called the Twelve Apostles, are in Port Campbell National Park off the coast of Victoria, Australia. Limestone, which is made mostly of carbon, plays a big role in Earth's carbon cycle.

Eventually, erupting volcanoes blast that carbon back into the atmosphere. Like the biological carbon cycle, the geological carbon cycle has no end and no beginning. Carbon simply moves through the cycle over and over again. But we'll start our look at the geological carbon cycle in the ocean.

Some sea creatures, such as phytoplankton and corals, use carbon and minerals from the water to build their protective shells. When these creatures die, their bodies sink to the seafloor. Over millions of years, the carbon and minerals in their shells turn into layers of limestone, which is made mostly of calcium carbonate. The limestone and the carbon it contains might remain trapped beneath the ocean floor for millions of years more.

But eventually the carbon starts moving again. And two tectonic plates—giant pieces of Earth's crust that hold the continents—collide with each other, shifting layers of limestone deep underground. When this happens, extreme heat from Earth's interior turns the minerals in limestone into magma (molten rock) and releases the carbon in limestone as a gas (carbon dioxide). As more magma accumulates underground, pressure builds.

THE GEOLOGICAL CARBON CYCLE

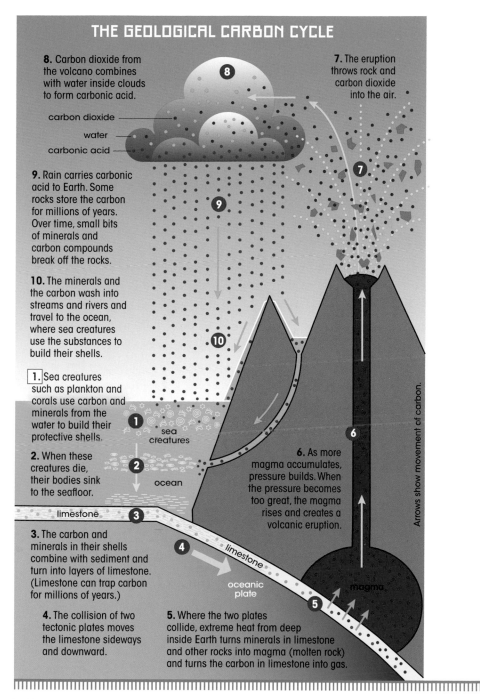

8. Carbon dioxide from the volcano combines with water inside clouds to form carbonic acid.

carbon dioxide ——
water ——
carbonic acid ——

9. Rain carries carbonic acid to Earth. Some rocks store the carbon for millions of years. Over time, small bits of minerals and carbon compounds break off the rocks.

10. The minerals and the carbon wash into streams and rivers and travel to the ocean, where sea creatures use the substances to build their shells.

1. Sea creatures such as plankton and corals use carbon and minerals from the water to build their protective shells.

2. When these creatures die, their bodies sink to the seafloor.

sea creatures

ocean

limestone

3. The carbon and minerals in their shells combine with sediment and turn into layers of limestone. (Limestone can trap carbon for millions of years.)

4. The collision of two tectonic plates moves the limestone sideways and downward.

5. Where the two plates collide, extreme heat from deep inside Earth turns minerals in limestone and other rocks into magma (molten rock) and turns the carbon in limestone into gas.

limestone

oceanic plate

magma

6. As more magma accumulates, pressure builds. When the pressure becomes too great, the magma rises and creates a volcanic eruption.

7. The eruption throws rock and carbon dioxide into the air.

Arrows show movement of carbon.

In the geological carbon cycle, carbon moves through the air, oceans, and Earth. It might remain underground for millions of years before being blasted back into the atmosphere during a volcanic eruption.

When the pressure becomes too great, the magma rises and creates a volcanic eruption. Steam, bits of rock, and carbon dioxide spray into the air.

Carbon dioxide from the volcano combines with water inside clouds to form carbonic acid. Rain carries carbonic acid back to the ground, where it eats away at rocks. Over time, small bits of minerals and carbon break off rocks and flow into rivers and eventually into the ocean, where the carbon cycle continues.

BREAKDOWN

The geological carbon cycle includes several built-in delays. Some kinds of rocks are natural carbon sinks. They absorb carbon from the rain and hold it, removing it for a time from the carbon cycle. Limestone, for instance, is made mostly of carbon. The carbon inside a limestone formation—whether it's aboveground, underwater, or deep inside Earth—remains there for millions of years. Some geologists want to enhance the geological carbon cycle to pull even more carbon out of the atmosphere. The geoengineering term for this is enhanced weathering.

Weathering is the gradual erosion and breaking apart of rocks. Biological weathering takes place when living organisms, such as plants and animals, wear down or break rocks. For instance, roots of a tree might grow into cracks in a rock. As the roots grow larger, they split the rock apart. Or an animal such as a rabbit or prairie dog might dig a burrow and might break up rocks. Even plantlike organisms such as algae and moss can break down rocks over time.

Another type of weathering, mechanical weathering, involves natural forces such as wind, ocean waves, or precipitation. Sometimes rainwater seeps into crevices in rocks, freezes into ice and expands, and breaks the rocks apart that way. Sometimes rocks break and smash into other rocks, breaking them up too. Rainfall plays a big part in rock weathering. Rain carries carbonic acid (carbon mixed with water). It eats away at rocks and breaks them apart. Different minerals in rocks react to carbonic acid at different rates. Very stable minerals, such as gold and quartz, may take hundreds of thousands of years to react to carbonic acid. Less stable minerals, such as silica, react and break down more quickly.

As rocks break down, bits of calcium, magnesium, and other minerals crumble off them and eventually wash into rivers and the ocean. Carbon compounds also break off the rocks and wash into the ocean. These are the compounds that certain sea creatures use to build their shells.

MESSING WITH MOTHER NATURE

What does any of this have to do with geoengineering and climate change? Every year, the geological carbon cycle pulls about 0.3 billion tons (0.27 billion metric tons) of carbon out of the atmosphere and stores it in the ocean. That amount is almost enough to offset the amount of carbon released into the atmosphere from other biological processes, such as plant and animal decay and animal respiration. If left alone, the biological carbon cycle and the geological carbon cycle pretty much regulate themselves, with the amount of carbon entering the atmosphere equaling the amount of carbon leaving the atmosphere.

The problem is that humans have disrupted the biological carbon cycle by cutting down forests and burning fossil fuels. The 0.3 billion tons (0.27 billion metric tons) removed during the geological carbon cycle don't even come close to offsetting the more than 9 billion tons (8.2 billion metric tons) of carbon that humans pump into the atmosphere each year.

But geologists say that perhaps we can use rocks to combat climate change. And not just any rocks. Geologists are looking at the rocks that trap the most carbon and considering how to use them to trap even more carbon.

SIMPLE SILICATES

The two most abundant elements in Earth's crust are oxygen and silicon. Together, they make up silicate rocks, which are almost 90 percent of the weight of Earth's crust. These rocks are also found on Earth's surface

Certain rocks, such as olivine, trap carbon dioxide at the bottom of waterways. Some engineers propose spreading large amounts of olivine along coastlines to absorb excess carbon dioxide.

and in its mantle, the layer of molten magma beneath the crust. Silicate rocks are extremely important to life on Earth because as they erode, they provide much needed nutrients for the soil, such as nitrogen and phosphorous. Without silicate rocks, plants and trees would not survive.

Of all the silicate rocks, it is the olivine that is most promising for geoengineering because it is naturally rich in magnesium. At the bottom of a river or ocean, magnesium in olivine reacts with water and traps carbon dioxide. So some engineers have proposed using large amounts of olivine to remove excess carbon from the atmosphere. They suggest mining olivine in mass quantities, breaking it up into small grains, and spreading it across vast stretches of land. The more olivine weathers and breaks up into tinier pieces of rock, the more it will react with rainwater and trap carbon dioxide. Some of the olivine grains will wash away in the rain to coastal rivers and oceans. But wherever the olivine ends up, it will carry carbon from the atmosphere with it.

According to Olaf Schuiling, a geochemist at Utrecht University in the Netherlands, the best place to put the olivine grains is on an ocean beach, where they will be exposed to not just rain but also pounding waves. The moving water will weather the olivine even faster, breaking it up into smaller and smaller slivers. And the more slivers of olivine, the more they will absorb carbon dioxide. An added benefit would be that olivine on a beach would quickly wash into the ocean, where it would store carbon indefinitely.

No one knows exactly how much olivine would be needed to trap significant amounts of carbon. One study showed that 2.2 pounds (1 kg) of olivine could store the equivalent weight of carbon dioxide. But another study concluded that 3 billion tons (2.7 billion metric tons) of olivine spread along the entire Amazon River basin would remove at the most 1 billion tons (0.9 billion metric tons) of carbon from the atmosphere.

One drawback of using olivine to capture carbon is that it would take a huge amount of energy to not only mine the rocks but also to pulverize them and spread them across the land. That energy would probably come from burning fossil fuels, which might wipe out the benefits of using olivine to capture carbon in the first place. Another drawback is that olivine contains the heavy metals nickel and chromium. While both are safe in small amounts, exposure to too much of these metals can sicken plants, animals, and humans. One laboratory study in the United Kingdom showed that an olivine particle crushed to the size of 1 micrometer (0.00004 inches), or about one-tenth the size of a water molecule, would take between one and five years to weather completely. As it weathered, it would add large amounts of chromium and nickel to the soil, threatening plant and animal life.

One of the benefits of using olivine to remove carbon from the atmosphere is that no elaborate storage system is needed. Olivine would simply carry carbon into sediments deep in the ocean. Adding extra olivine to the ocean would also reduce ocean acidification slightly. That would be useful because too much acid in the ocean, along with rising temperatures, is currently damaging coral reefs and other sea life. However, adding too much olivine to the ocean could drastically change the chemistry of seawater. This might harm the organisms living there. The ultimate goal in enhanced weathering is finding a solution that can take carbon from the atmosphere without harming the environment.

FIVE

CARBON IN THE WATER

THE OCEANS PLAY A BIG ROLE IN THE CARBON CYCLE.
Water absorbs carbon dioxide from the atmosphere, and living things in the ocean also take in carbon. For instance, microscopic sea creatures called phytoplankton pull carbon dioxide from the air during photosynthesis. Phytoplankton are not plants, but they make food the way plants do. They use a green pigment called chlorophyll to absorb sunlight. Then they combine sunlight with water and carbon dioxide to make food. The sun's rays can't penetrate deep into the ocean, so phytoplankton grow near the surface, where sunlight can reach them.

Phytoplankton use carbon in another way. They absorb carbon compounds from the water to make their protective outer shells. Other animals, including clams, oysters, and corals, also use carbon from the water to build their shells. When such creatures die, they fall to the seafloor. Over time, their carbon-filled shells turn into limestone. Trapped inside limestone, carbon can be sidetracked in the geological carbon cycle for millions of years. However, at any time, shifting tectonic plates might heat up the limestone and send the carbon it contains back into the air through volcanic eruptions. This is just one step in the ongoing geological carbon cycle.

ACID TESTS

The oceans are already enormous carbon sinks. They are responsible for absorbing almost 26 percent of the carbon that the burning of fossil fuels adds to the atmosphere. According to a study published in the journal *Earth System Science Data*, between 2002 and 2011, humans added about 9.3 billion tons (8.4 billion metric tons) of carbon to the atmosphere per year, and each year, the oceans absorbed almost 2.5 billion tons (2.3 billion metric tons) of that carbon.

Sea creatures such as clams, oysters, corals, and phytoplankton are part of the geological carbon cycle. They use carbon compounds from the water to build their protective shells. After the creatures die and fall to the seafloor, the carbon in their shells turns into limestone.

Oceans not only absorb carbon dioxide, but they also release it. Before people began burning vast amounts of fossil fuels, the amounts being absorbed and released were equal. Seawater normally contains a certain amount of acid, and before industrialization, that level was healthy

for sea life. But the burning of fossil fuels has released large amounts of nitrogen and sulfur into the air. These chemicals return to the oceans with rainwater, increasing ocean acidity and threatening the health of plants and animals in the water. Excess amounts of carbon dioxide, also from the burning of fossil fuels, increase ocean acidity even further.

So while the absorption of carbon dioxide by the oceans helps to offset carbon emissions from fossil fuels, it is also making the oceans more acidic. Since the Industrial Revolution, the acidity of the oceans has gone from 8.2 pH to 8.1 pH (pH stands for potential hydrogen, with a lower number equaling more acid). While a 0.1-pH drop might not seem like a lot, the pH scale is logarithmic, which means that pH 4 is ten times more acidic than pH 5 and one hundred times more acidic than pH 6. So a 0.1-pH drop represents an increase

Coral in this section of the Great Barrier Reef has bleached and died due to increased ocean temperatures and excess carbon dioxide in the water. The excess carbon makes the ocean too acidic for many plants and animals to survive.

in acidity of about 25 percent. The extra acidity is harming ocean ecosystems. Along with higher ocean temperatures, it is causing coral bleaching and killing fish, plants, and other sea life.

ALGAL BLOOMS: HARMFUL AND HELPFUL

Carbon dioxide isn't the only substance building up in Earth's waters. People are also adding vast amounts of nitrogen and phosphorus to rivers, lakes, and seas. These substances come from agricultural fertilizers that run off farm fields in the rain, wash into rivers, and eventually reach the ocean. Nitrogen and phosphorus, combined with sunlight and the excess heat brought on by global warming, nourish phytoplankton, causing phytoplankton populations to boom. These booming populations are called algal blooms. They can be small or enormous. The biggest ones can cover hundreds of square miles.

One of the largest algal blooms in recent history occurred in November 2015 in Lake Erie, between the United States and Canada. Caused by the runoff of phosphorous fertilizers, the sticky green bloom covered more than 300 square miles (777 sq. km) of the lake, an area about the size of the state of New York. Algal blooms such as this one harm the environment. Here's how it works: When the phytoplankton in an algal bloom die, they fall to the seafloor, where bacteria break them down. The bacteria consume most of the oxygen from the water, creating a dead zone where fish and other animals cannot survive. Algal blooms can also produce dangerous toxins that can kill fish and sicken humans who eat the contaminated fish.

Yet algal blooms are not all bad, at least when it comes to climate change. Since phytoplankton absorb carbon dioxide during photosynthesis and also to build their skeletons and since algal blooms consist of vast numbers of phytoplankton, algal blooms pull large amounts of carbon dioxide from the air. If biologists can figure out how to create algal blooms without harming ecosystems, they might be used as a weapon to fight climate change.

The plan is fairly simple. Scientists would fertilize the ocean with iron, a much needed nutrient for phytoplankton growth. The extra iron would trigger algal blooms. The science seems logical, but as is typical when humans interfere with nature, the outcomes are not completely predictable.

Marine biologists have conducted multiple experiments to test the theory of ocean fertilization. Victor Smetacek of the Alfred Wegener Institute for Polar and Marine Research in Potsdam, Germany, conducted one such experiment in 2012. His team added iron fertilizer, which is normally used to make lawns greener, to an eddy (a circular water current) in the Southern Ocean near Antarctica. The goal was to create a human-made algal bloom.

The experiment worked. A bloom appeared, turning the water from blue to turquoise, which indicated the large growth of phytoplankton. The bloom lasted for twenty-four days, during which Smetacek's team noticed a sharp decrease in dissolved carbon in the water and the atmosphere. The team assumed that the phytoplankton were absorbing carbon from the ocean and the air.

Algal blooms, such as this one in Kennedy Bay on New Zealand's North Island, threaten sea life by depleting oxygen supplies and sometimes producing toxins. But some scientists propose deliberately creating algal blooms because the phytoplankton they contain absorb large amounts of carbon dioxide during photosynthesis.

DIFFERENT FORMS OF CARBON

Carbon is found in air, oceans, rocks, soil, water, fossil fuels, and living things. Most of this carbon, however, is not in pure form (100 percent carbon). Instead, it consists of carbon atoms combined with other kinds of atoms. For instance, carbon dioxide is a gas combining carbon and oxygen. Calcium carbonate, or limestone, is a combination of calcium, carbon, and oxygen. Carbonic acid consists of water combined with carbon dioxide. Hydrocarbons, the main ingredients of petroleum and natural gas, are combinations of carbon and hydrogen. Inside living things, carbon can take various forms. For instance, glucose, a substance that stores energy in our bodies, is made of carbon, hydrogen, and oxygen. As carbon moves in the biological and geological carbon cycles, it combines with and separates from different substances along the way, taking different forms throughout its journey.

When the bloom died off, the phytoplankton fell to the bottom of the ocean, taking the carbon with them. Smetacek described the dead phytoplankton as "bits [that] settled on the seafloor as 'fluff' . . . like a layer of fluff that you would find under your bed if you did not vacuum it for a long time." He explained, "Eventually, this loose matter flattens into the sediments and a part gets buried; this stuff is sequestered [inside limestone] for geological time scales [hundreds of thousands to millions of years]."

The experiment seemed to be successful, since it showed that ocean fertilization is possible. However, Smetacek believes more research is needed before humans can use ocean fertilization on a grand scale. And even large-scale fertilization might not produce enough carbon absorption to offset the amount of carbon released by the burning of fossil fuels.

UPSETTING THE BALANCE

While ocean fertilization to increase algal blooms might sound like a promising idea, environmentalists warn about the repercussions of interfering with ocean ecosystems. Marine biologists say that phytoplankton are a key indicator of ocean health, and any shift in their populations can signal big environmental changes.

Climatologists know that Earth's oceans are warming due to climate change, but they don't know how warmer oceans will affect phytoplankton. One 2011 study published in a biological journal of the Royal Society in Great Britain found that phytoplankton in temperate zones of the ocean can adapt to warmer temperatures. But those in colder climates, near the North and South Poles, cannot adapt. This could mean that some phytoplankton will survive climate change while others will die.

Biologists are urgently trying to understand how climate change will affect phytoplankton because they are the food for many different ocean animals, including whales, snails, shrimp, jellyfish, and tiny zooplankton. Without phytoplankton, Earth's food chain—in which certain living things are eaten by other types of living things, which are themselves eaten by different types of living things—could break down. For example, without phytoplankton, zooplankton might starve. Without zooplankton, herring might starve. Without herring, tuna fish might starve. That would mean no tuna fish for humans. While humans might not starve if they couldn't eat tuna, other creatures in the food chain *would* starve. If the food chain suffers enough disruption, eventually humans would find their food sources greatly reduced.

Many biologists urge caution when considering making changes to the lowest member of the food chain. The relationships between the carbon cycle, the oceans, and ocean life are extremely complex. Scientists don't know how making alterations to these relationships will affect Earth and its inhabitants.

SIX

SHADING THE PLANET

ON JUNE 12, 1991, A HUGE CLOUD OF ASH AND GASES BLEW OUT OF THE TOP OF MOUNT PINATUBO, A VOLCANO ABOUT 54 MILES (87 KM) NORTHWEST OF MANILA, THE CAPITAL OF THE PHILIPPINES. The eruption was a strange and unexpected sight. Geologists had believed the volcano was dormant, or inactive, since it hadn't erupted in the previous five hundred years. But the stream of gases and ash wasn't the end of it. Three days later, on June 15, Mount Pinatubo erupted again. This time, the effect was devastating. An estimated 20 million tons (18 billion metric

Volcanic Mount Pinatubo, in the Philippines, explodes on June 12, 1991, sending millions of tons of ash, gas, and debris high into the atmosphere. The particles in the air reduced the amount of sunlight reaching Earth, leading to lower temperatures on the ground for more than two years. Scientists say that if we deliberately blasted particles into the air, we could imitate the effects of a volcano and reduce global temperatures to fight climate change.

tons) of gases, particles, bits of dirt, and rock burst violently into the air, forming a balloon-shaped cloud that measured more than 249 miles (401 km) across and rose more than 22 miles (35 km) above the ground. Avalanches of molten lava, ash, and rock fragments poured down the sides of the volcano, covering the surrounding area and killing more than three hundred people.

The eruption also had worldwide consequences. The stream of volcanic ash and gases shot all the way into the stratosphere. High in the air, winds carried the substances around the planet. Geologists from the Philippine Institute of Volcanology and Seismology and the US Geological Survey used satellites to track and measure the ash and gases as they traveled. What the researchers learned astounded them. They noted a decrease in global temperatures of almost 1°F (0.6°C) for more than two years after the eruption.

What had happened? Volcanic ash contains many different components: fine particles of dirt and rocks, plus gases such as water vapor, carbon dioxide, hydrogen sulfide, and sulfur dioxide. Blasted high in the air, particles from a volcano form dark clouds that can block out sunlight. And when sulfur dioxide from a volcano reaches the stratosphere, it combines with water to form tiny droplets of sulfuric acid. The droplets stick together to produce an aerosol—a fine mist— which can stay in the stratosphere for up to three years. This mist also reflects the sun's rays.

The combination of dark clouds and aerosols formed after a volcanic eruption cools Earth by blocking and reflecting sunlight, keeping it from reaching the ground. Climate scientists noted this cooling after the Mount Pinatubo eruption and realized that it might help solve Earth's climate change problems. The idea they proposed is called solar radiation management (SRM).

BOUNCE BACK

Like most other geoengineering concepts, SRM mimics a naturally occurring process. As the sun's rays enter Earth's atmosphere, about 30 percent of them immediately bounce back into space. The amount of solar radiation that returns to space is called the albedo. An increase in the albedo means that more radiation is being reflected. Larger albedo results in cooler global temperatures, since less heat from the sun reaches the surface of Earth. Climate scientists believe that by artificially increasing the albedo, they can drastically affect Earth's climate and reduce global warming.

One idea is to simulate the way volcanic particulates act in the stratosphere to reflect sunlight. To do this, some climate scientists propose injecting particles of sulfur dioxide into the stratosphere. While this happens naturally during volcanic eruptions, climate scientists don't know exactly how humans would pull it off.

BLACK AND WHITE

The albedo is a measure of how much of the sun's radiation is being reflected back into space. The measurement can range from a 0, or no reflection, to 1, which indicates 100 percent reflection. One of the best ways to increase the albedo at the surface of Earth is to simply change the colors of objects. Blacktop and asphalt roads, and most asphalt shingles, are black, a color that absorbs the sun's rays. By simply painting these surfaces a more reflective color, such as white, we can send more of the sun's rays bouncing back into the atmosphere. Studies show that using white or gray concrete instead of black asphalt for roads can increase the surface albedo by 50 to 70 percent. Ice and snow also increase the albedo because they are white. Soil, which is dark, has a much lower albedo. The albedo average for the planet as a whole is about 0.31. So Earth reflects about one-third of the radiation it receives from the sun.

Workers in Illinois pave a road using asphalt. The dark roadway will absorb a lot of the sun's rays and hold heat. In contrast, a white concrete road would reflect more of the sun's rays and stay cooler.

For instance, what size of particles should be used? Large particles might be too heavy and could fall out of the atmosphere instead of turning into aerosols. Small particles might have no effect at all. And how would we get the particles into the air? Should we take them there in airplanes or balloons? Should we shoot them into the sky using rockets and exploding shells?

Assuming scientists figure out all that, the result would be a sulfuric acid cloud in the stratosphere. It would remain in place until winds move it around. Eventually, like all clouds, the sulfuric acid cloud would degrade, or break apart. In one year, it would be one-third its original size. After two years, it would be two-thirds its original size. To maintain constant cloud cover and ongoing cooling of Earth, we'd need to continue injecting new sulfur dioxide into the atmosphere. Some climate scientists have suggested that we'd need to inject 1 to 5 million tons (0.9 to 4.5 million metric tons) of sulfur dioxide into the stratosphere every year to reduce global temperatures. That would require an immense number of planes, rockets, balloons, or other vehicles. Estimates of the annual cost are between $25 and $50 billion.

Besides the high price tag, the proposal has other drawbacks. Adding huge amounts of sulfur dioxide to the atmosphere may increase acid rain, which can damage plants on the ground and harm life in the oceans. And the extra sulfur dioxide might create holes in the ozone layer of Earth's atmosphere, allowing more of the sun's radiation to reach Earth.

Another big question is how to control the amount of cooling that would occur with this kind of SRM. The goal is to lower the overall global temperature, but only to a certain point. If too much of the sun's radiation is reflected, Earth could cool too rapidly. Finally, there is no way to predict exactly how clouds of sulfur dioxide will travel through Earth's atmosphere, where they will go, and how they will affect precipitation patterns and other weather events. No one knows exactly which regions will benefit from the shading and which might suffer.

OZONE ON EARTH

The ozone layer plays a big part in protecting Earth from solar radiation. It blocks the most harmful form of solar energy, ultraviolet rays. These could otherwise sicken and kill living things. In the 1970s, meteorologists discovered that between August and November each year, the ozone layer was thinning over Antarctica. Scientists measured reductions of almost 60 percent in ozone levels. They determined that chemicals called chlorofluorocarbons (CFCs), found in air conditioners, refrigerators, aerosol spray cans, and other consumer products, were rising through the atmosphere, combining with ice particles, and destroying some of the ozone in the stratosphere.

Journalists called the thinning of the ozone layer an ozone hole, although that was an exaggeration. The ozone layer did not have a gaping hole, but the thinning of the ozone was alarming nevertheless because it allowed harmful ultraviolet rays from the sun to reach Earth. Meteorologists discovered a smaller area of thinning ozone over the North Pole.

When meteorologists figured out that CFCs were depleting the ozone layer, governments around the world banned the chemicals. Manufacturers gradually phased them out and replaced them with chemicals that do not destroy ozone. According to NASA, which has been monitoring the ozone layer since the 1970s, the ozone layer above Antarctica still thins out once a year because of CFCs that remain in the atmosphere from before the ban, but the thinning is not as severe as it was in the 1970s. In fact, the ozone layer is thickening. Many meteorologists believe that it will be back to its normal thickness by 2100.

Thick clouds reflect the sun's rays back into space and reduce the amount of sunlight hitting Earth. One geoengineering idea involves deliberately thickening clouds to block sunlight and lower global temperatures.

Some models show that the technique might bring flooding to some parts of the globe while causing droughts in others.

IN THE CLOUD

Another SRM technique involves increasing the albedo using thick puffy clouds. These too would reflect the sun's rays and keep them from reaching Earth, thus cooling the planet. How do you make clouds big and puffy? One way is to seed them with acid. This makes the clouds produce more water vapor and makes them fluffier and more reflective.

Another option is called cloud brightening. It involves pumping seawater up into low-level clouds—between about 6,500 and 20,000 feet (1,981 to 6,100 m) above Earth. The salt in the seawater would increase the surface area of the water droplets within the clouds. With an increased surface area, the clouds would become more reflective, sending more light back into space. The salt particles would also make the clouds denser. A dense cloud takes longer to dissipate than an airy cloud, which means that it stays in the air longer, increasing albedo.

MIRRORS IN SPACE

One of the more aggressive forms of SRM involves placing one giant mirror or many tiny mirrors in space. The mirrors would move with Earth as it circled the sun, constantly reflecting the sun's light away from our planet.

Dr. David Keith, a physicist at Harvard University near Boston, Massachusetts, has proposed building a giant mirror out of strands of woven aluminum. It would look kind of like a massive window screen. The mirror wouldn't completely block sunlight. It would just filter it so that fewer rays reached Earth. Keith's theory is that if even 1 percent of the sun's rays were blocked, the mirror could fix Earth's climate troubles. The problem is that it would take a mirror roughly the size of Greenland to do the job. The logistics and cost of building a mirror that big and getting it into space make the idea impractical.

OCEAN BUBBLE BATHS?

Have you ever taken a whirlpool bath? The tiny bubbles that float to the surface of the water in whirlpool baths can actually reflect sunlight. Imagine taking this idea and magnifying it a million times or more to create a whirlpool bath in the ocean. Dr. Russell Seitz, a physicist at Harvard University, says that this approach could reduce the albedo and cool Earth.

While the idea doesn't include soap, Seitz says that by creating tiny bubbles in seawater, we could build "mirrors made of air." Computer models have shown that these microbubbles could decrease temperatures on Earth by as much as 5.4°F (3°C).

We could reflect sunlight away from Earth by launching one giant mirror or many small mirrors into orbit. Many scientists dismiss this kind of geoengineering program, since it would be extremely difficult to implement and manage, and the cost would be in the trillions of dollars.

In 2006 Dr. Roger Angel of the University of Arizona, one of the world's foremost experts on optics (the branch of physics dealing with the properties of light), suggested that instead of one giant mirror, we should deploy trillions of free-floating mirrors into space. The mirrors would work together to form a cloud that covered about half the diameter of Earth. A "cloud" of this magnitude would reflect about 2 percent of the sun's radiation. In Angel's proposal, each mirror would be about 2 feet (0.6 m) long and would weigh only as much as a butterfly. Angel has a plan for launching the mirrors into space over a span of ten years. The mirrors would be steered into position using solar power and would stay in place for up to fifty years.

Sounds a little like something you might see in a science fiction movie, right? That is what most other scientists think. The scientific community has shown little support for this kind of drastic maneuver, largely because no one knows how it would affect the planet. And the cost of creating and managing mirrors in space is estimated to be in the trillions of dollars. Still, support for this type of intervention is gradually increasing as the climate continues to heat up.

PROS—BUT EVEN MORE CONS

While SRM concepts are intriguing, most geoengineering advocates warn of drawbacks. They say that reflecting too much solar radiation could make Earth very cold, very quickly. It could also alter Earth's weather patterns in unpredictable ways. For instance, Dr. Piers Forster, a professor of climate change at the University of Leeds in the United Kingdom, writes, "All [SRM] mechanisms would . . . likely have harmful side effects in some regions, with much higher or much lower rainfall amounts in some regions." Increased acid rain and the creation of large ozone holes are other big risks. And using SRM to reduce the amount of sunlight coming to Earth's surface will directly harm solar power initiatives. With less sunlight, solar panels will collect less solar energy to convert into heat and electricity, making solar energy less effective as an alternative to fossil fuels.

One of the biggest concerns with SRM is that it does not remove carbon dioxide from the atmosphere. Forster says, "Solar radiation management doesn't change carbon emissions at all. It only reduces the planet's temperature or reduces its warming rate. Even with SRM, carbon emissions go on warming the planet and will increase if society doesn't change."

Then, with SRM, humans don't have to change their habits. They don't have to cut back on fossil fuel use. And some consumers might argue that if SRM can lower Earth's temperature back to normal, why use renewable energy? Why worry about how much carbon dioxide we are putting into the atmosphere?

That kind of thinking is not beneficial to the planet, climatologists say. Regardless of how much sun we might be able to reflect using SRM, reducing carbon emissions is crucial for the long-term health of the planet. Increased emissions don't just raise Earth's temperatures and alter its climate. They also cause smog, which is harmful to all living organisms. The excess carbon also alters the chemistry of ocean water and harms sea life.

Many scientists and government officials worry that if SRM measures are enacted, the push to reduce carbon emissions will disappear. People might abandon Earth-friendly initiatives, including the use of scrubbers that remove carbon dioxide from power plant smokestacks, eco-friendly electric cars, and reforestation efforts. Forster calls for a rational approach to solar radiation management. He says that SRM is "only worth considering if we also rapidly reduce CO_2 [carbon dioxide] emissions at the same time, otherwise any benefits would be quickly lost to CO_2 warming of the planet."

Then there's the question of whether SRM would be a practical, affordable long-term investment. SRM systems would be expensive to create and even more expensive to maintain. Computer models indicate that once any type of SRM is in place, the program would need to continue indefinitely. The models show that stopping SRM would cause an abrupt and drastic increase in the global temperature, possibly with devastating effects on Earth and its inhabitants.

Although it is controversial and might be dangerous, some researchers continue to explore the possibility of SRM. Advocates of SRM argue that it is a quick way to get the global climate issue under control. They note that while SRM may seem a bit scary, the reward might be worth the risk and should at least be investigated.

SEVEN

GEOENGINEERING OUR FUTURE

THE WORLD RUNS ON ENERGY. We used it every day to fuel our cars, heat our homes, and run our factories. As the global population increases, so too does energy consumption. The world's population is predicted to rise from the 2010 level of seven billion to nine billion people by 2040. According to the report *BP Energy Outlook* of 2016, worldwide energy consumption is expected to increase by 34 percent between 2014 and 2035. The largest consumers of energy over those years are predicted to be China and India, as both of their economies grow and develop.

Yet even as the world's population booms, an interesting trend is appearing. In 2012, 2013, and 2014, global energy consumption grew at a much smaller pace than expected. In previous years, energy consumption grew by 2.3 percent a year. But the growth rate was just 1.4 percent in 2012, 1.8 percent in 2013, and 0.9 percent in 2014. And people are using more renewable energy. The BP report estimates that by 2035, renewable energy might make up more than 16 percent of total global energy consumption. More renewables means less air pollution and fewer greenhouse gas emissions.

RENEWABLE EXPECTATIONS

If renewable energy is so good for the planet, why aren't more countries calling for a complete conversion to renewables? The truth is that renewables aren't the perfect solution to our energy problems. Most have limitations that make them difficult to implement on a worldwide scale. They're often less reliable than fossil-fuel-based energy. Modern

Power lines, such as these running through the California wilderness, carry electricity to consumers whenever they need it, twenty-four hours a day. Much of the electricity generated in the United States comes from burning coal, a fossil fuel.

power systems are set up to supply a constant amount of energy to consumers as it's needed. Electricity that comes from burning coal, for instance, is delivered to customers day or night, whenever they turn on a light or a machine. By contrast, harvesting solar power is only possible during the daytime when the sky is clear. During the night and on stormy or very cloudy days, solar panels cannot collect any sunlight. Were power companies to switch from coal to solar power, they would not be able to supply this energy at any time of day or night. Similarly, if winds are calm, turbines can't harness wind power. Energy converters cannot capture ocean energy if the ocean has very little wave action.

Renewable energy also costs more than power from fossil fuels. For instance, while the price of installing and maintaining solar panels on a home has come down in recent years, it can still cost $25,000 to $35,000 to install a home solar system. Cars that run on electricity or

Some Americans are cutting fossil fuel use by installing solar panels or solar roof shingles on their homes. Solar energy can cost more than power from fossil fuels, but as solar technology improves, costs will likely decrease.

hydrogen power are also more expensive than cars that run on gasoline. And charging stations for electric cars and refueling stations for hydrogen cars are few and far between. That makes it difficult for car owners to power up their vehicles as needed.

As more companies get behind renewable energy, and as more governments offer tax breaks and other incentives for its use, costs should come down. But switching from fossil fuels to renewables will take time. Even with the switch to more renewables, carbon emissions are expected to grow by 20 percent from 2014 to 2035. Around the world, government and business leaders are struggling to confront this reality.

PLANNING FOR THE FUTURE

In 2015 the United Nations Environment Programme held its twenty-first annual Conference of the Parties in Paris. Commonly referred to as COP21, this conference brought together more than twenty-five thousand delegates, representing individual countries, the United Nations, nongovernmental agencies, and scientific organizations from around the world. The goal was to reach an international agreement on the most effective methods of combatting climate change. COP21 focused on getting countries to commit to an increase of no more than 3.6°F (2°C) in global warming by the end of the century. That goal will require governments to invest more heavily in renewable energy and to implement carbon reduction programs.

At the end of the conference, representatives of 195 nations signed a legally binding agreement "to combat climate change and unleash actions and investment towards a low carbon, resilient and sustainable future" and to limit the global climate temperature increase to only 2.7°F (1.5°C) by the end of the twenty-first century. Participating nations will aim to reach net-zero carbon emissions by the end of the twenty-first century. Net-zero emissions occurs when the amount of carbon entering the atmosphere equals the amount of carbon leaving the atmosphere.

The agreement didn't specifically address geoengineering. In fact, international leaders are divided on whether geoengineering is a good way to handle climate change. Opponents say that geoengineering is a drastic and potentially harmful option for reducing global temperatures, but others feel that it should be investigated.

UNANSWERED QUESTIONS

Making large-scale changes to any system, particularly one as huge as Earth, will leave some kind of impact. That means that all the geoengineering technologies outlined so far need to be assessed for their

PROFIT MOTIVES

At the moment, most geoengineering technologies are in their early development. Companies will have to invest a great deal of money on these projects to get them off the ground, with no guarantee that they'll eventually make a profit. Yet as interest in and research on geoengineering grows, businesses are increasingly likely to get on board.

Private companies—including large energy companies such as ExxonMobil and Royal Dutch Shell—are already pouring millions of dollars into geoengineering research. While this research might lead to lower temperatures on Earth, it might also lead to big profits for the companies. But some commentators question their motives, suggesting that energy companies are putting money behind SRM because it promises to lower global temperatures without asking consumers to reduce fossil fuel use. The big energy companies make billions of dollars each year by extracting and selling fossil fuels. Reduced use of fossil fuels would cut into company profits. So it makes sense that energy companies might support SRM but not more Earth-friendly efforts to reduce carbon emissions.

risks and costs. Scientists have experience with certain technologies, such as planting forests and seeding clouds, so anticipating results will be easier. Other techniques, such as placing mirrors in space, enhanced weathering, and burning biomass, have little or no hands-on research to back them up. Engineers must rely solely on computer modeling to anticipate the results of these techniques.

But computer models are not always accurate. It is tough to code a program to allow for the many variables in nature. For example, much of the computer modeling to show how aerosols move through the stratosphere comes from studies of the eruption of Mount Pinatubo. Were another volcano to explode tomorrow, the aerosols might take a different path through the atmosphere. Real-life events do not always mimic computer models.

All types of geoengineering come with questions of right and wrong. Some argue that it is morally wrong for humans to mess with nature using geoengineering. They say that people caused the climate crisis in the first place and that people should remedy it by protecting the natural world instead of interfering with it further. "Improving nature conservation [protecting plants and animals] is what we should do in order to fight climate change, not trying to change nature," said François Simard of the International Union for Conservation of Nature in 2010. The US Environmental Defense Fund warns of the unintended consequences of geoengineering. "Deliberate climate interventions such as albedo modification should not be undertaken for the foreseeable future as they present serious ecological, moral and geopolitical concerns," the group states on its website.

No one can say exactly what the environmental and political consequences of geoengineering might be, but some researchers have made predictions. Some say that solar radiation management might disrupt the monsoons of Southeast Asia. These are seasonal winds that bring extremely heavy rains to that part of the world every summer. The people of Southeast Asia depend on these rains for water. If geoengineers interfere with the monsoons, "between 1.2 and 4.1 billion people could be adversely affected by changes in rainfall patterns," says Piers Forster. He warns that parts of the region could drastically dry out, turning into a desert. Other models predict that inserting aerosols into the stratosphere will cause a drought in the Amazon region.

What happens if these predictions come true? Could disruptions in global ecosystems lead to crop failure and famine? Wars over dwindling supplies of water? Millions of refugees fleeing drought-stricken or flooded regions? No one knows.

And what if a nation were to use geoengineering techniques to damage its enemies, as the United States did during the Vietnam War? Although the United Nations has prohibited the use of weather modification in warfare, governments have not completely abandoned the idea. "[Other countries] are engaging even in an eco-type of terrorism whereby they can alter the climate, set off earthquakes [or trigger] volcanoes remotely through the use of electromagnetic waves," US defense secretary William Cohen reported at a conference on global terrorism in 1997. Dr. Alan Robock, a climate scientist at Rutgers University in New Jersey, claims that in the twenty-first century the US Central Intelligence Agency, a government spy organization, has worked with climatologists on plans to manipulate the weather to harm enemy nations. But if the CIA, the military, or another government group had such a plan, it would probably not make that information public.

PROCEED WITH CAUTION

While geoengineering is extremely controversial, many climatologists argue that we have no choice but to continue investigating its use. Geoengineering researcher Matt Watson of the University of Bristol in the United Kingdom says, "Personally I find this stuff [geoengineering] terrifying but we have to compare it to doing nothing, to business-as-usual leading us to a world with a [7.2°F, or 4°C, temperature] rise."

David Keith says, "There are lots of very good arguments for and against solar geoengineering but there's little doubt that it could alter global average temperature. The question is how good a job it would (or would not) do at reducing other climate risks such as changes in rainfall and sea-level rise." The US National Academy of Sciences also has mixed feelings about geoengineering. In a 2015 report, it noted, "Climate intervention is not a replacement for reducing carbon emissions." The report stated that "proposed intervention techniques are not ready for wide-scale employment." Yet this same body recommended further research into geoengineering projects.

Alan Robock assesses the situation this way: "Would it be more dangerous to do it or to not do it? That's the question." Robock goes on to say that being in favor of researching geoengineering is not the same thing as supporting its implementation. The National Research Council, which is part of the National Academy of Sciences, concurs. It believes we must examine all our options in the face of the climate crisis.

Even if scientists and politicians can all agree on the need for geoengineering, there is not yet a global plan for implementing it. A global plan is a necessity because many geoengineering techniques, such as SRM and enhanced weathering, would affect the entire planet.

And currently, no global governing body is in charge of overseeing geoengineering. At global geoengineering conferences, attendees have discussed rules for the how's and why's of implementing climate engineering but have not yet agreed on any firm rules. Who should set the guidelines? Who would oversee implementation and maintenance of projects? Who would pay for initiatives that cost billions or trillions of dollars? Finally, who would compensate the victims if geoengineering leads to unintended consequences, such as famine or war? So far, these crucial questions remained unanswered.

WHAT'S NEXT?

With geoengineering still in the research phase and with no concrete plans for implementation yet under way, how can people cope with

Waves break against a seawall at Stanley Park in Vancouver, British Columbia. As sea levels rise around the world, more and more communities are adapting by building seawalls to protect beaches and buildings along the coast.

rising temperatures on Earth, as well as the floods, droughts, and other weather events exacerbated by climate change? The answer is adaptation. Biologists might develop genetically modified crops that can thrive in warmer climates. Engineers might improve irrigation systems in newly drought-stricken areas and create flood defenses in coastal areas to protect the land from rising seas. To help people cope with decreased water supplies, builders might install rainwater-capture systems on the roofs of houses. Farmers might grow crops that can survive with low amounts of water.

While most scientists say that people will need to adapt to climate change, that doesn't mean they should give up on trying to fight it. Climatologists, government leaders, and others agree that every person on Earth should be looking for ways to keep climate change in check. Richard Houghton suggests, "People, including kids, can plant trees.

BREAKING IT DOWN

Dr. Clare Heyward is a political scientist at the University of Warwick in the United Kingdom. She believes that the terms *climate engineering* and *geoengineering* can scare people because the idea of humans altering Earth's climate can seem a bit sinister. Instead, she proposes that we talk about five different approaches to fighting climate change: mitigation, carbon dioxide removal, solar radiation management, adaptation, and rectification.

Mitigation means taking specific actions to reduce the amount of greenhouse gases we put into the atmosphere. Mitigation can include the use of renewable energies, a reduction in fossil fuel use, and other eco-friendly activities.

Carbon dioxide removal refers to taking carbon dioxide out of the atmosphere. Methods might include reforestation, enhanced weathering, ocean fertilization, and direct carbon capture.

Solar radiation management aims to decrease global temperatures by reducing the amount of sunlight reaching Earth. Techniques include placing mirrors in space, spraying aerosols into the stratosphere, and increasing albedo at Earth's surface.

Adaptation refers to people adjusting to life in a warmer world. To adapt, people might build seawalls to protect coastlines from flooding, grow different kinds of crops, or even move to new areas to escape droughts or floods caused by climate change.

Rectification deals with any negative results of geoengineering technology. For example, suppose the United States sprayed aerosols into the stratosphere to cool Earth but that resulted in another country experiencing severe drought or floods. The United States would have to rectify, or compensate for, that damage, perhaps by paying the nation it affected.

People can try to use less energy by being more efficient in energy use (insulation, natural lighting, and weatherizing). Most importantly, people can insist on their governments' creating incentives for energy conservation and use of renewable energy." Piers Forster recommends that people of all ages "change their family behavior." He suggests that families consider driving electric cars and using alternative fuels.

You can do your part to cut down on fossil fuel consumption by walking or biking to school instead of taking a car. If you can't get to your school without a vehicle, carpool with others or take public transportation. When you ride-share, more people travel on the same amount of fuel.

You can also reduce fossil fuel use and fight pollution by using less plastic. Some of the chemicals used to make plastics are toxic. Most plastics are made from petroleum or natural gas. Extracting these substances from the ground and turning them into products involves emissions of both carbon and methane, greenhouse gases that contribute to climate change. You can cut down on your use of plastic by taking reusable cloth bags to the grocery store and drinking water from ceramic mugs instead of plastic bottles.

You can help in reforestation efforts by volunteering with a tree-planting project. Contact a group such as TreePeople, the Arbor Day Foundation, or the Alliance for Community Trees to see how you can join in. You can find a group near you by typing the name of your state or city into a search engine, along with key words such as *tree planting* and *volunteers*.

Finally, you can contact government leaders, including representatives in your state legislature and the US Congress. To find your federal representatives' contact information, including phone numbers and e-mail addresses, go to the website Common Cause and click on "Find Your Lawmakers." Ask them what they're doing to fight climate change, and tell them your views. If you are old enough to vote, vote for candidates with strong platforms on combatting

Members of Richmond Trees, a volunteer organization in Richmond, California, pose for a photo after planting a young tree on a neighborhood street. Tree planting is one way that communities can work to fight climate change.

climate change. Go online to learn about the candidates in upcoming elections. If you like what they stand for, you can even volunteer to work on their campaigns.

Climatologists warn that climate change will affect every aspect of our lives. As atmospheric carbon levels continue to rise, people around the world will have no choice but to grapple with higher temperatures, fiercer storms, rising sea levels, and other life-altering environmental changes. Peter Eisenberger of Global Thermostat predicts, "How we adjust to [climate change] will reshape the important part of living in the twenty-first century." Will that adjustment include geoengineering? Only time will tell.

SOURCE NOTES ||||||||||||||||||||||||||||||||||||||||||||||||||||||||||||||||||||||||||||||||||||||||||

7   Jacob Brogan, "What's the Deal with Geoengineering?," *Slate*, January 6, 2016, http://www.slate.com/articles/technology/future_tense/2016/01/can _we_stop_climate_change_by_tinkering_with_the_atmosphere.html.

9   Jay Zwally, "Jay Zwally Warns Greenland Ice Loss Is Canary in Coal Mine," EarthSky, February 22, 2010, http://earthsky.org/earth/jay-zwally-warns-loss -of-greenland-ice-is-canary-in-coal-mine.

26   Silvio Marcacci, "7 Interesting Global Renewable Energy Trends from NREL (Charts Galore!)," *CleanTechnica*, January 26, 2015, http://cleantechnica .com/2015/01/26/7-interesting-global-renewable-energy-trends-from-nrel -charts-galore/.

28   Vincent Schaefer, quoted in Matt Novak, "Weather Control as a Cold War Weapon," *Smithsonian.com*, December 5, 2011, http://www.smithsonianmag .com/history/weather-control-as-a-cold-war-weapon-1777409/?no-ist.

39   Dr. Richard Houghton, e-mail message to author, April 5, 2016.

44   Daniel Kammen, quoted in Robert Sanders, "Electricity from Biomass with Carbon Capture Could Make Western US Carbon-Negative," *Berkeley News*, February 9, 2015, http://news.berkeley.edu/2015/02/09/electricity-from -biomass-with-carbon-capture-could-make-western-u-s-carbon-negative/.

59   Victor Smetacek, quoted in Wynne Perry, "Could Fertilizing the Oceans Reduce Global Warming?," *Live Science*, July 18, 2012, http://www.livescience .com/21684-geoengineering-iron-fertilization-climate.html.

68   Russell Seitz, quoted in Smriti Rao, "Could Turning the Oceans into a Giant Bubble Bath Cool the Planet?," *80 Beats* (blog), March 29, 2010, http://blogs .discovermagazine.com/80beats/2010/03/29/could-turning-the-oceans-into-a -giant-bubble-bath-cool-the-planet/#.Vx-NpvkrJD_.

70   Dr. Piers Forster, e-mail message to author, April 12, 2016.

70   Ibid.

71   Ibid.

75   "Historic Paris Agreement on Climate Change," United Nations Framework Convention on Climate Change, December 12, 2015, http://newsroom .unfccc.int/unfccc-newsroom/finale-cop21/.

77   François Simard, quoted in Chisa Fujioka, "UN Urged to Freeze Climate Geo-engineering Projects," Reuters, October 21, 2010, http://www.reuters .com/article/us-geoengineering-idUSTRE69K18320101021.

77   "Our Position on Geoengineering," Environmental Defense Fund, accessed February 2, 2017, https://www.edf.org/climate/our-position-geoengineering.

78   Piers Forster, quoted in David Shukman, "Geo-engineering: Climate Fixes 'Could Harm Billions,'" *BBC News*, November 26, 2014, http://www.bbc.com/news/science-environment-30197085.

78   William Cohen, quoted in J. D. Heyes, "Weather Weapons Have Existed for Over 15 Years, Testified US Secretary of Defense, *Natural News*, June 6, 2013, http://www.naturalnews.com/040652_weather_weapons_chemtrails_HAARP.html.

78   Matt Watson, quoted in Shukman, "Geo-engineering Climate Fixes."

79   Dr. David Keith, e-mail message to author, April 27, 2016.

79   National Academies of Sciences, Engineering, and Medicine, "Climate Intervention Is Not a Replacement for Reducing Carbon Emissions," news release, National Academies of Sciences, Engineering, and Medicine, February 10, 2015, http://www8.nationalacademies.org/onpinews/newsitem.aspx?RecordID=02102015.

79   Alan Robock, quoted in Nell Greenfieldboyce, "Scientific Pros Weigh the Cons of Messing with Earth's Thermostat," *National Public Radio*, February 10, 2015, http://www.npr.org/sections/thetwo-way/2015/02/10/385065816/scientific-pros-weigh-the-cons-of-messing-with-earths-thermostat.

80, 82 Houghton, e-mail.

82   Forster, e-mail.

83   Dr. Peter Eisenberg, telephone conversation with author, April 8, 2016.

GLOSSARY

acid rain: rain or snow with higher than normal levels of acidic compounds, such as sulfuric acid and nitric acid. The compounds come from air pollution, mix with water vapor inside clouds, and fall as precipitation. When it reaches lakes, rivers, and soil, acid rain can kill fish and other wildlife. Acid can also eat away at the surface of buildings, bridges, and other structures.

aerosol: a mixture of extremely small particles or droplets suspended inside gas. In the air, aerosols can take the form of smoke, mist, fog, or clouds. Some particles in aerosols, such as volcanic ash and pollen, enter the atmosphere naturally. Other particles enter the air when people burn fossil fuels. High in the atmosphere, aerosols reflect sunlight back into space. So some climate scientists propose inserting aerosols into the stratosphere to fight global warming. The aerosols would deflect sunlight, leading to lower temperatures on Earth.

albedo: a measure of how much of the sun's radiation is being reflected back into space. The measurement can range from a 0, or no reflection, to 1, or 100 percent reflection. Different surfaces on Earth, such as clouds, ice caps, and oceans, have different albedos. The albedo average for the planet as a whole is about 0.31, so Earth reflects about one-third of the radiation it receives from the sun.

atmosphere: the layer of gases surrounding Earth or another planet. Some of the gases, such as carbon dioxide, methane, and water vapor, trap heat near the planet. As people have burned more and more fossil fuels, atmospheric carbon dioxide levels have risen, trapping more heat and leading to climate change on Earth.

biochar: charcoal produced by the burning of plant matter for fuel. Some environmentalists propose placing large amounts of biochar on farm fields, where it will absorb rainwater, keep the soil moist, and help crops grow. Then the carbon inside biochar will simply remain there, not moving into the atmosphere to increase carbon levels.

biomass: organic matter that can be burned as fuel, such as leaves, sticks, grass, wood chips, and bark. Because plants practice photosynthesis and absorb carbon dioxide, biomass contains carbon. When biomass is burned, it releases this carbon back into the atmosphere. The amount of carbon taken from the atmosphere during photosynthesis and released into the atmosphere during burning cancels itself out. So we say that biomass is carbon neutral.

carbon cycle: the series of natural and industrial processes by which carbon travels through the environment. In the natural carbon cycle, carbon moves through the air, rocks, soil, volcanoes, clouds, rain, the oceans, and the bodies of plants and animals in an endless loop. In the natural cycle, atmospheric levels of carbon remain steady. However, by extracting fossil fuels from deep underground and burning them, people have increased atmospheric carbon levels.

carbon dioxide: a colorless and odorless greenhouse gas vital to life on Earth. All green plants use carbon dioxide to make food. Animals produce carbon dioxide when they convert food into energy. Carbon dioxide is a greenhouse gas—it traps the sun's heat near Earth. Excess carbon dioxide in the atmosphere, caused by the burning of fossil fuels, has led to higher temperatures on Earth.

carbon neutral: having net-zero carbon emissions by taking out of the atmosphere the same amount of carbon that is released into the atmosphere

carbon sink: an area that absorbs large amounts of carbon dioxide from the atmosphere. Natural carbon sinks include forests, oceans, soil, and rocks.

climate change: in the modern era, the warming of Earth's atmosphere caused by the burning of fossil fuels. The release of heat-trapping carbon dioxide into the atmosphere has altered Earth's climate and led to more extreme weather, including droughts, floods, and ferocious storms.

cloud brightening: a proposed geoengineering technique that involves pumping seawater into low-level clouds. The salt in the seawater would increase the surface area of the water droplets in the clouds. With more surface area, the clouds would become more reflective and send more of the sun's light back into space. The result would be lower temperatures on Earth.

cloud seeding: adding particles or gases to a cloud to cause it to precipitate, or make rain or snow. Farmers sometimes use cloud seeding to bring rain to a specific area. Nations have also used cloud seeding during warfare to flood enemy lands.

ecosystem: an ecological community consisting of interdependent biological and physical entities. The biological members of an ecosystem are the plants and animals that live there. The physical members are elements such as air, soil, water, and weather. Members of an ecosystem interact with and depend on one another. For instance, certain plants in an ecosystem might serve as food for certain animals.

erosion: natural processes such as water flow and wind that carry soil and rock from one location on Earth to another. Erosion can damage an ecosystem. For instance, strong winds might carry off rich topsoil from farm fields, leaving them dry and dusty. Without a layer of topsoil, fields cannot absorb rainwater needed to nourish plants.

evaporation: the process by which liquid water changes into water vapor, or water in gas form. Evaporation occurs when water is heated. Rising temperatures on Earth, caused by heat-trapping gases in the atmosphere, are leading to increased evaporation.

fossil fuels: fuels formed inside Earth from the remains of ancient plants and animals. Coal, petroleum, and natural gas are examples of fossil fuels. They contain carbon from the long-dead bodies of the plants and animals from which they formed. When people burn fossil fuels, that carbon enters the atmosphere.

geoengineering: the deliberate large-scale manipulation of Earth's climate. Some scientists propose using geoengineering to halt or reverse human-made climate change and global warming. Proposed geoengineering techniques include cloud brightening, carbon capture and sequestration, and deflecting sunlight by using mirrors in outer space.

greenhouse gas: a gas that traps heat in Earth's atmosphere. Examples include carbon dioxide and methane. Human activities such as the burning of fossil fuels have released extra greenhouse gases into the atmosphere, leading to global climate change.

limestone: a rock composed mainly of calcium carbonate. Many marine animals, including corals, oysters, and clams, use calcium carbonate from the water to build their shells and bones. After they die, over millions of years, the calcium carbonate in their bodies turns into limestone.

meteorologist: a scientist who studies weather and the atmosphere

ozone layer: a region of Earth's stratosphere that holds a thick band of ozone. This layer of gas absorbs harmful radiation from the sun. By absorbing this radiation, the ozone layer protects life on Earth.

particulates: microscopic particles and droplets of liquid suspended in Earth's atmosphere. Particulates can combine with moisture in the air to form smog, a type of air pollution.

photosynthesis: the process by which plants, algae, and some other organisms use sunlight, carbon dioxide, and water to make food. Large areas covered with plants, such as forests, absorb vast amounts of carbon from the air to use in photosynthesis. When people cut down forests, fewer plants are left to absorb carbon.

phytoplankton: plantlike organisms that live at or near the surface of oceans, lakes, and other bodies of water. Phytoplankton are important to the carbon cycle in two ways. First, they practice photosynthesis—they absorb carbon dioxide from the atmosphere to make food. Phytoplankton also use calcium carbonate from the water to build their protective shells. After they die, the carbon in their bodies turns into limestone. Carbon stored in limestone might remain underground or underwater for millions of years.

reforestation: planting new trees in areas where forests have been destroyed or in places where trees haven't grown before. Reforestation might help fight climate change because trees in forests absorb so much carbon dioxide to use in photosynthesis.

renewable energy: fuel that replaces itself naturally or that never runs out. Examples include biomass, since people can grow new plants to replace those burned for fuel. Another example is solar power, since the sun will keep shining for billions of years.

SELECTED BIBLIOGRAPHY

"Accelerated Ice Melt Causing Iceland to Rise." *Discovery News*, February 3, 2015. http://news.discovery.com/earth/global-warming/accelerated-ice-melt-causing -iceland-to-rise-150103.htm.

"Air Pollution." *National Geographic*. Accessed May 3, 2016. http://environment .nationalgeographic.com/environment/global-warming/pollution-overview.

Anderson, Allison. "School-Based Reforestation to Combat Climate Change." Brookings Institution, June 3, 2011. http://www.brookings.edu/research /opinions/2011/06/03-school-based-reforestation-anderson.

Biello, David. "Coral Reefs Show Remarkable Ability to Recover from Near Death." *Scientific American*, January 15, 2015. http://www.scientificamerican.com/article /coral-reefs-show-remarkable-ability-to-recover-from-near-death/.

Brewer, Peter G., and James Barry. "Rising Acidity in the Ocean: The Other CO2 Problem." *Scientific American*, September 1, 2008. http://www.scientificamerican .com/article/rising-acidity-in-the-ocean/.

Brogan, Jacob. "What's the Deal with Geoengineering?" *Slate*, January 6, 2016. http:// www.slate.com/articles/technology/future_tense/2016/01/can_we_stop_climate _change_by_tinkering_with_the_atmosphere.html.

Butler, Rhett. "10 Facts about the Amazon Rainforest." Mongabay.com. Last modified January 23, 2016. http://rainforests.mongabay.com/amazon/amazon-rainforest -facts.html.

"Case Study: Drought in the Sahel." *BBC*. Accessed May 2, 2016. http://www.bbc .co.uk/schools/gcsebitesize/geography/water_rivers/drought_rev3.shtml.

"Climate Change Causes: A Blanket around the Earth." NASA. Accessed May 2, 2016. http://climate.nasa.gov/causes/.

"Climate Modification Schemes." American Institute of Physics, June 2011. https:// www.aip.org/history/climate/RainMake.htm.

Coonan, Clifford. "How Beijing Used Rockets to Keep Opening Ceremony Dry." *Independent* (London), August 10, 2008. http://www.independent.co.uk/sport /olympics/how-beijing-used-rockets-to-keep-opening-ceremony-dry-890294.html.

Cressey, Daniel. "Rock's Power to Mop Up Carbon Revisited." *Nature.com*, January 21, 2014. http://www.nature.com/news/rock-s-power-to-mop-up-carbon -revisited-1.14560.

"Earth's Energy Budget." NASA. Accessed May 2, 2016. http://earthobservatory.nasa .gov/Features/EnergyBalance/page4.php.

Fares, Robert. "Renewable Energy Intermittency Explained: Challenges, Solutions, and Opportunities." *Scientific American*, March 11, 2015. http://blogs .scientificamerican.com/plugged-in/renewable-energy-intermittency-explained -challenges-solutions-and-opportunities/.

"Forests and Carbon Storage." US Forest Service. Accessed May 3, 2016. http://www
.fs.usda.gov/ccrc/topics/forests-and-carbon-storage.

Gertner, Jon. "The Secrets in Greenland's Ice Sheet." *New York Times*, November 12,
2015. http://www.nytimes.com/2015/11/15/magazine/the-secrets-in-greenlands
-ice-sheets.html.

"Global Climate Change: Albedo." Earth System Science Education Alliance. Accessed
April 5, 2016. http://essea.strategies.org/module.php?module_id=99.

"Global Greenhouse Gas Emissions Data." EPA. Accessed May 2, 2016. http://www3
.epa.gov/climatechange/ghgemissions/global.html#three.

Goldenberg, Suzanne, John Vidal, Lenore Taylor, Adam Vaughan, and Fiona Harvey.
"Paris Climate Deal: Nearly 200 Nations Sign in End of Fossil Fuel Era." *Guardian*
(US ed.), December 12, 2015. http://www.theguardian.com/environment/2015
/dec/12/paris-climate-deal-200-nations-sign-finish-fossil-fuel-era.

"The Greenhouse Effect." EPA. Accessed May 2, 2016. http://www3.epa.gov
/climatechange/kids/basics/today/greenhouse-effect.html.

Hannam, Peter. "Global Warming: Australian Deserts to Expand as Tropical Circulation
Changes." *Sydney Morning Herald*, February 24, 2015. http://www.smh.com.au
/environment/climate-change/global-warming-australian-deserts-to-expand-as
-tropical-circulation-changes-20150223-13n121.html.

Harris, Richard. "This Climate Fix Might Be Decades ahead of Its Time." *National
Public Radio*, June 27, 2013. http://www.npr.org/2013/06/27/189522647/this
-climate-fix-might-be-decades-ahead-of-its-time.

Horton, Jennifer. "How Can Adding Iron to the Oceans Slow Global Warming?"
HowStuffWorks, March 31, 2008. http://science.howstuffworks.com
/environmental/green-science/iron-sulfate-slow-global-warming1.htm.

"How Earth-Scale Engineering Can Save the Planet." *Popular Science*, June 22, 2005.
http://www.popsci.com/environment/article/2005-06/how-earth-scale
-engineering-can-save-planet.

"How Volcanoes Influence Climate." University Corporation for Atmospheric Research.
Accessed May 3, 2016. http://scied.ucar.edu/shortcontent/how-volcanoes
-influence-climate.

"The Importance of Forests." WWF. Accessed May 3, 2014. http://wwf.panda.org
/about_our_earth/deforestation/importance_forests/.

Johnson, Scott K. "A Not-So-Modest Proposal to Remove Atmospheric Carbon Dioxide."
Ars Technica, December 22, 2015. http://arstechnica.com/science/2015/12/a-not
-so-modest-proposal-to-remove-atmospheric-carbon-dioxide/.

Jones, Nicola. "Solar Geoengineering: Weighing Costs of Blocking the Sun's Rays." *Yale Environment 360*, January 9, 2014. http://e360.yale.edu/feature/solar_geoengineering_weighing_costs_of_blocking_the_suns_rays/2727/.

Keith, David. "A Cheap but Dangerous Global Warming Fix." *PBS*, July 16, 2015. http://www.pbs.org/newshour/making-sense/cheap-controversial-solution-climate-change/.

Kintisch, Eli. "Amazon Rainforest Ability to Soak Up Carbon Dioxide Is Falling." *Science*, March 18, 2015. http://www.sciencemag.org/news/2015/03/amazon-rainforest-ability-soak-carbon-dioxide-falling.

———. "Can Sucking CO2 out of the Atmosphere Really Work?" *MIT Technology Review*, October 7, 2014. https://www.technologyreview.com/s/531346/can-sucking-co2-out-of-the-atmosphere-really-work/.

Klusinske, Elizabeth. "Geoengineering to Combat Climate Change: Carbon Dioxide Removal." Decoded Science, April 28, 2015. http://www.decodedscience.org/geoengineering-combat-climate-change-carbon-dioxide-removal/53960.

Marcacci, Silvio. "7 Interesting Global Renewable Energy Trends from NREL (Charts Galore!)." *CleanTechnica*, January 26, 2015. http://cleantechnica.com/2015/01/26/7-interesting-global-renewable-energy-trends-from-nrel-charts-galore/.

Matthews, John A., ed. "Stratospheric Aerosol Injection (SAI)." *Encyclopedia of Environmental Change*, 2014. doi:10.4135/9781446247501.n3730.

Monroe, Rob. "How Much CO2 Can the Oceans Take Up?" Keeling Curve, July 3, 2013. https://scripps.ucsd.edu/programs/keelingcurve/2013/07/03/how-much-co2-can-the-oceans-take-up/.

National Center for Scientific Research. "Weathering of Rocks Impacts Climate Change," news release, February 29, 2012. http://www2.cnrs.fr/en/1995.htm.

Novak, Matt. "Weather Control as a Cold War Weapon." *Smithsonian.com*, December 5, 2011. http://www.smithsonianmag.com/history/weather-control-as-a-cold-war-weapon-1777409/?no-ist.

Perry, Wynne. "Could Fertilizing the Oceans Reduce Global Warming?" *Live Science*, July 18, 2012. http://www.livescience.com/21684-geoengineering-iron-fertilization-climate.html.

Powell, Alvin. "Geoengineering: Opportunity or Folly?" *Harvard Gazette*, October 29, 2013. http://news.harvard.edu/gazette/story/2013/10/geoengineering-opportunity-or-folly/.

Rao, Smriti. "Could Turning the Oceans into a Giant Bubble Bath Cool the Planet?" *80 Beats* (blog), March 29, 2010. http://blogs.discovermagazine.com/80beats/2010/03/29/could-turning-the-oceans-into-a-giant-bubble-bath-cool-the-planet/#.Vx-NpvkrJD_.

Ravilious, Kate. "From Forestry to Geoengineering, Silicate Weathering Counts." Environmental Research Web, June 27, 2012. http://environmentalresearchweb .org/cws/article/news/50085.

Robock, Alan, Allison Marquardt, Ben Kravitz, and Georgiy Stenchikov. "Benefits, Risks, and Costs of Stratospheric Geoengineering." Wiley Online Library, October 2, 2009. http://onlinelibrary.wiley.com/doi/10.1029/2009GL039209/full.

Sanders, Robert. "Electricity from Biomass with Carbon Capture Could Make Western US Carbon-Negative." *Berkeley News*, February 9, 2015. http://news.berkeley .edu/2015/02/09/electricity-from-biomass-with-carbon-capture-could-make -western-u-s-carbon-negative/.

Schiller, Jakob. "Beautiful Polar Photos Tell a Haunting Story about Climate Change." *Wired*, November 11, 2014. http://www.wired.com/2014/11/camille-seaman -melting-away/.

Seewer, John. "Feds: Lake Erie Algae Bloom in 2015 Was Largest on Record." *Phys.org*, November 10, 2015. http://phys.org/news/2015-11-feds-lake-erie-algae-bloom.html.

Shulman, Seth. "Momentum Builds for Deforestation-Free Palm Oil." *Live Science*, March 8, 2014. http://www.livescience.com/43962-deforestation-free-palm-oil.html.

"Space Sunshade Might Be Feasible in Global Warming Emergency." *ScienceDaily*, November 5, 2006. https://www.sciencedaily.com/releases/2006/11 /061104090409.htm.

"State of the Cryosphere." National Snow and Ice Data Center. Last modified November 9, 2015. https://nsidc.org/cryosphere/sotc/ice_sheets.html.

"What Is US Electricity Generation by Energy Source?" US Energy Information Administration. Accessed May 3, 2016. https://www.eia.gov/tools/faqs/faq .cfm?id=427&t=3.

Williamson, Phil. "Emissions Reduction: Scrutinize CO2 Removal Methods." *Nature. com*, February 10, 2016. http://www.nature.com/news/emissions-reduction -scrutinize-co2-removal-methods-1.19318.

Worland, Justin. "Climate Change Is Making the Land in Iceland Rise." *Time*, February 2, 2015. http://time.com/3691920/climate-change-iceland/.

Zwally, Jay. "Jay Zwally Warns Greenland Ice Loss Is Canary in Coal Mine." EarthSky. org, February 22, 2010. http://earthsky.org/earth/jay-zwally-warns-loss-of -greenland-ice-is-canary-in-coal-mine.

FURTHER INFORMATION

BOOKS

Chazdon, Robin. *Second Growth: The Promise of Tropical Forest Generation in an Age of Deforestation*. Chicago: University of Chicago Press, 2014.

Goldstein, Margaret J. *Fuel under Fire: Petroleum and Its Perils*. Minneapolis: Twenty-First Century Books, 2016.

Goodell, Jeff. *How to Cool the Planet: Geoengineering and the Audacious Quest to Fix Earth's Climate*. Boston: Mariner Books, 2011.

Hamilton, Clive. *Earthmasters: The Dawn of the Age of Climate Engineering*. New Haven, CT: Yale University Press, 2013.

Hand, Carol. *Dead Zones: Why Earth's Waters Are Losing Oxygen*. Minneapolis: Twenty-First Century Books, 2016.

Heos, Bridget. *It's Getting Hot in Here: The Past, Present, and Future of Climate Change*. Boston: HMH Books for Young Readers, 2016.

Hirsh, Rebecca. *Climate Migrants: On the Move in a Warming World*. Minneapolis: Twenty-First Century Books, 2017.

Kallen, Stuart A. *Running Dry: The Global Water Crisis*. Minneapolis: Twenty-First Century Books, 2015.

Kintisch, Eli. *Hack the Planet: Science's Best Hope—or Worst Nightmare—for Averting Climate Catastrophe*. Hoboken, NJ: Wiley, 2010.

McPherson, Stephanie Sammartino. *Artic Thaw: Climate Change and the Global Race for Energy Resources*. Minneapolis: Twenty-First Century Books, 2015.

Morton, Oliver. *The Planet Remade: How Geoengineering Could Change the World*. Princeton, NJ: Princeton University Press, 2015.

Ride, Sally, and Tam E. O'Shaughnessy. *Mission Planet Earth: Our World and Its Climate—and How Humans Are Changing Them*. New York: Flash Point, 2009.

Simpson, Kathleen. *Extreme Weather: Science Tackles Global Warming and Climate Change*. Washington, DC: National Geographic, 2008.

FILM AND VIDEO

A Climate of Change. DVD. Los Angeles: Participant Media, 2009. This documentary focuses on everyday people working to fight climate change—from students in India who protest the overuse of plastic to villagers in Papua New Guinea trying to save their rain forests to West Virginians speaking out against environmentally destructive coal-mining practices. Award-winning actress Tilda Swinton narrates the film.

"How Geoengineering Could Change the World." YouTube video, 1:11:06. Talk by Oliver Morton, Town Hall, Seattle, January 25, 2016. Posted by "talkingsticktv," January 27, 2016. https://www.youtube.com/watch?v=TjJ5ZE5WmNg. In this video lecture, science writer Oliver Morton discusses ways to remove carbon dioxide from the atmosphere, including reforestation and fertilizing oceans with iron. He also explains how humans might be able to cool Earth by reflecting more sunlight away from the planet, for example by brightening clouds. Finally, he examines the challenges and potential dangers of using such techniques.

Human Footprint. DVD. Washington, DC: National Geographic, 2008. This film follows the typical American through a lifetime, chronicling that individual's impact on Earth. The "human footprint" includes all the plastic and other garbage people throw away, the fossil fuels we burn, the trees we cut down, and the carbon dioxide we add to the air. The end result is environmental devastation.

WEBSITES

The Canopy Project
http://www.earthday.org/campaigns/reforestation/the-canopy-project/
Sponsored by the Earth Day Network, the Canopy Project is working to restore ecosystems and fight climate change by planting forests around the world. Since launching in 2010, the project has planted more than 1.5 million trees in twenty-one countries.

Clean Technica
http://cleantechnica.com/
The Clean Technica website offers articles and statistics on alternative energy technology, including solar power, wind power, biomass, and electric cars.

Corals and Coral Reefs
http://ocean.si.edu/corals-and-coral-reefs
This website from the US National Museum of Natural History introduces corals, how they live and reproduce, and how they grow together to create coral reefs. The site also discusses how climate change is damaging coral reefs and what people can do to protect them.

Global CCS Institute
https://www.globalccsinstitute.com/
Based in Australia, the Global CCS Institute focuses on developing and testing carbon capture and storage systems, a technology that might be able to reduce levels of atmospheric carbon. The group's website includes articles on CCS projects around the world.

Global Climate Change: Vital Signs of the Planet
http://climate.nasa.gov/
This website from the National Aeronautics and Space Administration offers statistics on atmospheric carbon dioxide levels, global temperatures, and the melting of ice in polar regions. The website also includes articles about climate change, climate-science activities for kids, and educational videos.

INDEX

PHOTO ACKNOWLEDGMENTS

The images in this book are used with the permission of: © iStockphoto.com/
lovelyday12 (leaf background); © Cindy Hopkins/Alamy, p. 7; © Laura Westlund/
Independent Picture Service, pp. 9, 11, 13, 17, 35, 36, 49; © Jon Arnold Images
Ltd/Alamy, p. 19; © Daniela Dirscherl/WaterFrame/Getty Images, p. 22; © Kevork
Djansezian/Getty Images, p. 24; © Hero Images/Getty Images, p. 25; © inga spence/
Alamy, p. 29; AP Photo/Ng Han Guan, p. 30; © Kevin Frayer/Getty Images, p. 33;
© Enrique Molina/age fotostock RM/Getty Images, p. 38; © Universal Images Group/
Getty Images, p. 40; © Victor de Schwanberg/Alamy, p. 42; © In Pictures Ltd./Corbis/
Getty Images, p. 43; © MICHAEL URBAN/AFP/Getty Images, p. 45; © UIG//
Getty Images, p. 48; © Wilson44691/Wikimedia Commons (license type), p. 52;
© iStockphoto.com/Gfed, p. 55; AP Photo/Kike Calvo, p. 56; © David Wall/Alamy,
p. 58; © ARLAN NAEG/AFP/Getty Images, p. 62; © Daniel Acker/Bloomberg/Getty
Images, p. 64; © iStockphoto.com/kavram, p. 67; © visdia/Shutterstock.com, p. 69;
© iStockphoto.com/Pgiam, p. 73; © B Christopher/Alamy, p. 74; © Will Datene/First
Light/Getty Images, p. 80; © Richard Wong/Alamy, p. 83.

Front cover: © iStockphoto.com/lovelyday12.

ABOUT THE AUTHOR

Science rocks! And so do Jennifer Swanson's books. She's the award-winning author of
more than twenty-five nonfiction science books for kids. *Geoengineering Earth's Climate*
is her first title for Twenty-First Century Books. Curious about the world, Swanson
started a science club in her garage at the age of seven. She now lives in Florida and
teaches middle school science. You can find out more at her website,
www.JenniferSwansonBooks.com.